BRIGHT NOTES

IVANHOE AND OTHER WORKS BY SIR WALTER SCOTT

Intelligent Education

Nashville, Tennessee

BRIGHT NOTES: Ivanhoe and Other Works
www.BrightNotes.com

ISBN: 978-1-645424-02-4 (Paperback)
ISBN: 978-1-645424-03-1 (eBook)

Originally published by Monarch Press.
Richard Dunlavey, 1964
2020 Edition published by Influence Publishers.

Interior design by Lapiz Digital Services. Cover Design by Thinkpen Designs.

Printed in the United States of America.

Library of Congress Cataloging-in-Publication Data forthcoming.
Names: Intelligent Education
Title: BRIGHT NOTES: Ivanhoe and Other Works
Subject: STU004000 STUDY AIDS / Book Notes

CONTENTS

INTRODUCTION TO SIR WALTER SCOTT

No man was ever more fortunate in the time and place of his birth than Sir Walter Scott. He was a Scot at a time when Scottish arts and sciences flourished as they never had or would again. Hume in philosophy, Adam Smith in Economics, Sir Humphry Davy in Science, and writers like Thomson, Boswell, Smollett, and Burns, were part of the illustrious tradition into which Scott was born in 1771. His early education was slight, but his mind grew up on the **ballads** and stories of Scotland's glorious past. He heard many of them for the first time while recovering from a children's disease (probably infantile paralysis) at his grandfather's farm. His illness also gave him the opportunity to read a great deal, and his discovery of Bishop Percy's *Reliques* (old English ballads) at the age of twelve awakened him to the possibilities of a similar collection of Scottish balladry. In time he returned to his native Edinburgh to study law, and was admitted to the bar in 1792. But his antiquarian interests prevailed, and in that same year he began a series of annual ballad-hunting expeditions to the countryside. The fruits of these travels appeared first in 1802-3 in his Minstrelsy of the Scottish Border, and later in seven long narrative poems by his own hand.

Beginning in 1805 with the *Lay of the Last Minstrel*, these brisk tales of border wars and wonders established Scott's reputation as a poet. *Marmion* (1808) retold the notorious defeat of Scottish chivalry at Flodden Field in grim Gothic tones; *The Lady of the Lake* (1810) was a picturesque tale, full of local color and customs, concerning a disguised king who travels among his enemies. (Note, in both works, a foreshadowing of *Ivanhoe.*) Upon these three poems Scott, a contemporary of Coleridge and Wordsworth at the height of their powers, built a wider fame than any English poet of his generation.

In 1812 Lord Byron's *Childe Harold's Pilgrimage* appeared, and overnight a youth of twenty-four had replaced Scott as England's first poet. His equipment was comparable to Scott's, but he dramatized the sufferings and passions of his characters unlike the older, more conservative poet. Scott's own *Bridal of Triermain and Rokeby* the following year hastened the decline of his fame. Pressed by financial obligations, notably the construction of a family estate at Abbotsford, Scott wisely returned to complete the twice-discarded manuscript of a novel, and published it anonymously in 1814 as *Waverley*. Once more his stock began to rise (his authorship was common gossip well before he admitted it publicly in 1827). Although he wrote two more verse tales, a life of Napoleon, and several volumes of short fiction, essays, etc., the remainder of his career is remembered for the monumental production of his thirty-two novels. Apart from literature, it is remembered also as the period of Scott's greatest suffering and personal triumph as a man. Despite the enormous success of the novels, the expense of Abbotsford and a business collapse in 1825 wiped out Scott's fortune. Rather than declare bankruptcy he was able to repay nine shillings to the pound (nearly half) on a debt of about 130,000 pounds, by turning out novels with incredible industry and regularity for six hard years. He cleared his name and relieved his beloved Abbotsford of all debts, but at the expense of his health. He died at Abbotsford in 1832 at the age of 62.

THE WAVERLEY NOVELS

The thirty-two *Waverley* novels (so-called because all were attributed to the anonymous "author of Waverley") stand as a milestone of English literature. Their bulk alone is staggering, but Scott's achievement is as varied as it is large. During the nineteenth century his popularity was built upon the historical romances: *Ivanhoe, Quentin Durward, The Talisman,* etc. Alongside this vogue grew the misconception that Scott's range as a novelist was narrow, that he was simply a medievalist content with a serene vision of a past too remote and perfect to be real. One look at a list of his total production will dispel this fallacy. Many of his novels are set in the seventeenth and eighteenth centuries, and two (*The Antiquary* and *St. Ronan's Well*) are nearly modern. It is true that he preferred Scottish settings and characters, but several of his books travel to the continent-one as far as Palestine. Another kind of breadth is apparent in his characterizations. His best characters are spread across the entire face of society, from Madge Wildfire, an impoverished madwoman, to heads of state like Louis XI of France, and the Moslem Sultan, Saladin.

CATEGORIES

One convenient method of classifying the *Waverley* novels is to divide them chronologically according to date of composition into two groups: the nine Scottish novels of 1814-19, and the historical romances. Those written before *Ivanhoe* are set in Scotland at a time not much earlier than the present. Among these *The Heart of Midlothian* is generally esteemed as Scott's finest book; and *Rob Roy* has always been a favorite. Starting with *Ivanhoe* in 1820, Scott broke new ground in setting, time, and tone. Many regard this shift as the beginning of a decline in the quality of his work that continued to his death. The enduring appeal of *Ivanhoe* has made it the best-known and most influential of Scott's works. It is the first novel of the second group; *Quentin Durward*, another medieval tale, is probably the best.

STYLE

In his heyday, Scott wrote twenty of his best books over a period of eleven years: nearly two a year between 1814-15. It follows that Scott, who wrote many other things during these years, was a hasty and careless writer. His daily work quota amounted to thirty printed pages, and he claimed to have written two-thirds of *Waverley*, his first novel, inside of two weeks. As a result there are errors and contradictions in detail in even his best books. His prose style is flabby and tedious to the modern ear. He often bores us with long, involved sentences, too many of which never quite make grammatical sense. Digressions are frequent-descriptions of architecture, costumes, and landscape, for example, interrupt his action continually. His plots are slipshod and seem to have been improvised as he went along. As a rule his stories are slow getting started and interminable as they drag toward a foregone conclusion. There is a limit to the faults we can blame on hasty composition, however. The moral issues that he raises seem superficial and unreal, and his heroes and heroines lack depth and interest, as a rule.

Rather than prolong this catalogue of faults we must ask why, despite them, Scott's name survives along with a substantial part of his work. Why do we read him at all? One answer is that his name has not survived in any meaningful sense, that the development of the novel since Scott's day has relegated his books to the shelf of heavy, unread "classics." When the grain of truth in this is admitted, the fact remains that Scott continues to entertain and charm vast numbers of adult readers. Despite the heavy style in which they are written, Scott's historical romances are among the most stirring and unforgettable stories in English. If nothing else, Scott knew how to tell a story (after all, his models were Homer, Shakespeare, and Ariosto). The elaborate costumes and architectural descriptions are as appealing to the sympathetic reader of Scott as the shield of Achilles is to a fancier of Homer. Indeed, they frequently help to enrich our sense of setting and social history. As for characters, it is true that Scott rarely saw beneath the surface of their actions-but what a surface he did see! The very superficiality of his characters makes it possible for him to focus on their manners and gestures, to show us how they appeared to others in their society. He is at his best with lower-class Scottish characters whose dialects and eccentricities he copied with great skill and affection. His comic figures are often successful; and the gallery of fine historical portraits in the Waverley novels is impressive. If his heroes and heroines seem pale, we must remember that such "good" characters are always the hardest to make interesting. It is to Scott's credit that he ever succeeded with them; yet Jeanie Deans (*The Heart of Midlothian*) and Rebecca (*Ivanhoe*) are among his masterpieces.

THE HISTORICAL NOVEL

Scott's innovations in the novel form have a great deal to do with the permanence of his fame. Unquestionably his most significant contribution was the invention of the modern historical novel. Many had made the attempt before Scott, but their works failed, either from dullness, unreality, or sensationalism, to recapture the mood of the past. Using the techniques Fielding and Smollett had applied to modern life, Scott set his stories in the past. He invented characters and projected their stories against some great historical event, with great men in secondary roles whenever possible. He loaded his books with descriptions and paid particular attention to the customs and peculiarities of the time. He modified the dialogue of his characters to the closest modern equivalent of their actual speech. At its best this method produced a sense of having lived in the past. Making good use of the traditions of the eighteenth century novel and the resources of his own imagination, therefore, Scott set the fashion in historical fiction for a century to come.

SCOTT'S INFLUENCE

Scott's influence on later writers was extensive. His romances captured the imagination of a generation of Europeans who memorialized their esteem for him with flattering imitations and even non-literary tributes like The Abduction of Rebecca (a famous painting by Delacroix) and *Lucia di Lammermoor* (Donizetti's opera). England and America responded with Bulwer-Lytton, James Fennimore Cooper, Dickens, Hawthorne, Kingsley, Thackeray, and Stevenson-all tried their hand at Scott's new form in the spirit he had pioneered. The continent produced Hugo, Merimee, and Dumas in France; Gogol and Tolstoy in Russia; and numerous others in Italy and Germany. Besides their literary importance, the *Waverley* Novels also had an impact upon political life during the nineteenth century. The revolutionaries in Europe's emerging nation-states took heed of Scott's patriotism. His portrait of Scotland's past glories stimulated them to do the same in their countries, as a means of establishing or reawakening a sense of national pride in their people. A third area in which Scott left his mark was historical writing itself. Dull chronicles and lifeless compilations of fact gave way to a new and vivid kind of history in the nineteenth century. Spearheaded by such students of Scott as Carlyle, Prescott, macaulay and Parkman, history became the story of the past, a recreation of the spirit of the time, as well as an account of its events. Even in religion, Scott helped touch off the Oxford movement in England by his celebration of a ritualistic past when men and morals were better than they are today. There was, in short, little about European life that did not feel the effect of Scott's novels.

SCOTT'S PLACE IN ROMANTICISM

Scott was the most popular writer in the Romantic period (ca. 1798-1825) and a cardinal influence in the spread of Romantic ideas and feelings. By rescuing the Middle Ages from the shadows of mystery and terror he came to be regarded by some as "the middle point and culmination of English Romanticism" (Beers). Scott, Ernest Baker observes, opened up the dimension of time for his generation just as Byron was to open up geography. Yet Scott seems to have had nothing else in common with the movement he led than an interest in the past. Even at that, he was interested for vastly different reasons. To poets like Keats, Wordsworth, and Coleridge, the Middle Ages were a refuge for troubled minds; a time when the Industrial Revolution and the Napoleonic Wars had not yet been heard of and men were free and uncorrupted. For Scott it was a gimmick for repeating the success of his Scottish novels. (If anything, he was more concerned with the similarities between past and present than their differences.) He had run out of Scottish materials and feared that he would lose his public if he did not try a new approach. Beyond this Scott seems to have been an eighteenth century man in all respects. For the most part he disliked what the Romantic poets were doing (Coleridge, and perhaps Byron, excepted). He saw no need to return to the language of real speech in order to trace the fundamental laws of human nature. Dialect interested him well enough for its sound and charm, but for no deeper reason. Otherwise his prose was as ponderous as Samuel Johnson's, his dialogue as formal as Milton's. Nature, the Romantic idol, did not interest him on its own account; he saw no immanent deity or "sense sublime of something far more deeply interfused" in "rocks, and stones, and trees." He disapproved of extremes of emotion; intuition seemed to him a poor substitute for common sense; and he never cared for artistic egotism. A Romantic strictly by adoption, Scott "brought to bear on romantic materials a mind humorous and worldly-wise, extrovert and sane."

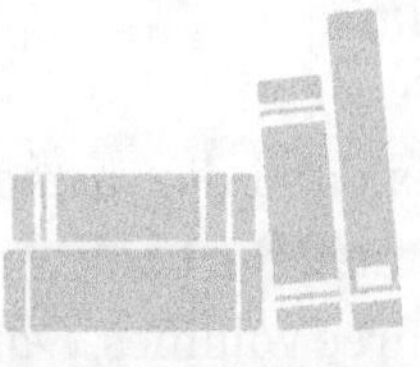

INTRODUCTION TO IVANHOE

IVANHOE

Scott's own introduction to the 1830 edition of his novels is the best account of the genesis of *Ivanhoe*. He had fared extremely well with the Scottish novels, but now he wanted to change his formula. Why should he be typed as a "Scottish" novelist? Why couldn't he look elsewhere for the materials of his art? The obvious direction in which to move was South-to England. *The Heart of Midlothian* and *Rob Roy* both had had English scenes, but *Ivanhoe* was the first of Scott's novels set entirely in England. Scott says the idea of his story was suggested by a second-rate tragedy named *Runnamede*. The name of *Ivanhoe* is from an old **ballad** about a dispute between Lord Hampden and the Black Prince (son of Edward III):

Tring, Wing, and Ivanhoe, For the striking of a blow, Hampden did forego, And glad he could escape so.

Front-de-Boeuf had a more likely origin in the Auchinleck manuscript roll of ancient English names. And the **episode** in Friar Tuck's cell was suggested by "the disguised expeditions of Haroun Alraschid," the caliph of the *Arabian Nights*. Oddly enough, Scott's rather bright tale was written during a painful illness. He had been bedridden because of stomach cramps during the winter of 1818, and was so weak and distracted by agony that he could not hold a pen; so he dictated the book to a secretary. Published on December 18, 1819, in three volumes, *Ivanhoe* quickly outsold any of his earlier novels-12,000 copies, an unparalleled commercial success. Scott had become possibly the first best-seller in literature and reached the high-tide of his popularity. After Scott, novelists needed have no shame for their genre, or doubts about the possibility of making a living by their art.

SOURCES

Aside from *Runnamede* and the random sources Scott acknowledged in his introduction, several additional ones should be noted. A number of characters and incidents are drawn directly from life. Rebecca is modeled after a Philadelphia lady, Rebecca Gratz, described to Scott by Washington Irving, the American humorist. The idea of using Jewish characters in the book grew out of a conversation between Scott and Skene and Rubislaw. And the Templar's miraculous death seems to have occurred to Scott after witnessing Mr. Elphistone of Glack fall dead in the Edinburgh Parliament. Most of Scott's specific literary debts, from Homer to Goethe, have been cited in the commentary after the chapter summaries following. In general, Scott's narrative approach derives from the English novel from as he inherited it. He has Fielding's eye for human peculiarity and his fondness for concealed identities and surprise endings. With Smollett he shares a love of Scotland, and especially of the Scottish character and idiom. Mrs. Radcliffe's landscapes, which reflect and harmonize with the mood of her novel's action, occasionally appear to good advantage in Scott. She, together with the other prominent traffickers in horror and mystery fiction ("Gothic" novelists), may be held to account for Scott's feeble attempts in this vein. Of Jane Austen, Scott's greater contemporary, it can be said that he admired her work, but he seems to have learned nothing from her. More useful, no doubt, was the failure of Queenhoo Hall, a historical novel by Strutt, which Scott finished and published in 1808.

Other sources include Homer, Shakespeare, Ariosto, Chaucer, and Goethe. Chaucer provided the portrait of Prior Aymer; Goethe and Schiller lent one or two specific episodes. Ariosto was the "pattern" for Scott's sprawling narrative. Shakespeare, like Scott an adapter of history, seems never to have been out of Scott's mind. To Homer's *Odyssey* he owes the general plot of a homecoming hero, disguised to prevent premature identification, recognized by a swineherd, and eventually successful in restoring peace to his nation and order to his household. Like the *Iliad, Ivanhoe* derives its main plot interest from the abduction and attempted rescue of a beautiful woman. In fact Scott repeats this **episode**: once for Rowena, once for Rebecca. Like the siege of Troy, the siege of Torquilstone succeeds because of treachery within the walls. And even Rebecca's report of the battle to Ivanhoe reminds us of Helen's enumeration of Achaian warriors for Priam high atop the walls of Troy. These resemblances and even the many Homeric **similes** in *Ivanhoe* are merely the concrete evidence of a much larger debt that Scott, like all writers of heroic adventure, owes to Homer.

HISTORICAL BACKGROUND

The entire action of *Ivanhoe* takes place in 1194, the year of King Richard's return to England from the Crusades. It is set in the counties of Yorkshire, Nottinghamshire, and Leicestershire, with Sherwood forest at its center. Below are some additional facts that will supply the information Scott assumed his readers to have.

THE NORMAN CONQUEST

For several centuries after the end of the Roman occupation, Britain was occupied by Germanic and Scandinavian invaders. These intruders drove many of the Celtic natives to the North and West and intermarried with the remainder to produce a race of Anglo-Saxons, or simply Saxons. The Saxons regarded themselves as the sovereign owners and rulers of their adopted land. They instituted a monarchy and began to develop a distinct culture of their own. In the eleventh century, however, a dispute arose over the succession to the English throne. The death of Edward the Confessor in 1066, with no legitimate heir to succeed him, left the field wide open. The strongest candidate was Harold, a powerful Saxon lord, and he ascended the throne in that same year. But the ruler of French-speaking Normandy across the channel, Duke William, felt he had a clearer title than Harold and got most of continental Christendom to agree. While Harold was repelling a Norwegian invasion in the autumn of 1066, William landed his army on the British mainland. The two met at Hastings in an **epic** battle that was to shape the course of British history. William became "the Conqueror," by beating Harold and replacing the Saxon way of life with Norman. Hence the bitter antagonism between Norman and Saxon upon which Scott's novel is based became inevitable and lasted for many generations. But the persistence of a Saxon claim to the English throne throughout the next century is entirely Scott's invention.

CRUSADES

Another important aspect of *Ivanhoe* is Prince John's plot to usurp King Richard's throne. The opportunity for his treason was Richard's departure for the Third Crusade to Palestine (1090-

1093), a united attempt of the major powers in Christendom to rid the Holy Land of Moslem occupation. Richard took with him the flower of English knighthood but left behind the powerful Norman barons and his brother John to rule in his stead. Many of these barons, hoping to increase their own power during Richard's absence, saw in John an agreeably weak successor to Richard, and therefore backed his conspiracy to the hilt. On his return from the Crusade, Richard was imprisoned in Austria from December 1192, to January 1194. During his captivity he earned the name "Lion-hearted" (Coeur-de-Lion) by tearing out the heart of a lion sent to devour him.

KNIGHTLY ORDERS

The coincidence of religious and military interests during the Crusades gave rise to an unusual occupation: the warrior-priest. Like most of the clergy of the time, they were organized into Holy Orders, the most famous being the Templars and the Hospitallers. The Order of Knights Templars (or Holy Order of the Temple of Zion) was formed in Jerusalem in 1128 and named after their headquarters in the Temple of Solomon. (See Chapter XXXV for the rule of their Order.) Their purpose was to protect pilgrims to the Holy Land from Saracens, and during the Third Crusade they fought bravely in defense of the Holy Sepulcher. In 1312 the Order was discontinued, either because of the impiety and moral deterioration that Scott describes in Chapter XXXV, or because they had grown too wealthy and powerful. A similar Order, the Knights Hospitallers, or Knights of St. John, appeared at about the same time as the Templars. The rivalry between them is nicely illustrated in the flare-up between Aymer and Bois-Guilbert in Chapter V.

MEDIEVAL CHRISTIANITY

The history of the Catholic Church during the medieval period is a tale of expanding power, decline and reform. Most of what is now Western Europe was bounded, not by national frontiers, but by Christendom. France, Italy, and Germany did not exist as distinct entities. Cultural and even political differences between nations were secondary to the Christian beliefs they held in common. Latin, the universal language of the church, was the standard tongue throughout Christendom. In such a world the Catholic clergy held enormous power and this power often bred corruption. When one group or Order of monks began to moulder, however, another Order would spring up to correct its errors. One of the great reforming Orders was the Benedictines, who lived a harsh, monastic life. When they themselves began to weaken, a stricter Order, the Cistercians, was formed within the Benedictine ranks (1098). By the time *Ivanhoe* opens, even this reform within reform had decayed to the point where a man like Aymer could rise to become Prior in one of its monasteries. At the opposite extreme from formal church government and institutions stands Friar Tuck, the "hedge-priest." (See Scott's note on this.) This character is one of the many historical inaccuracies in *Ivanhoe*, since mendicant (or begging) friars did not exist in the twelfth century.

MEDIEVAL JEWRY

When Jews began to emigrate to Western Europe in the Middle Ages they were greeted with hostility and contempt. To Europeans they were no better than the Saracens who defiled the sacred relics of Christ in Palestine. They looked outlandish, spoke gibberish, and believed in a strange God. It was they who had crucified the Savior. One result of this kind of thinking in

England, was widespread persecution of Jews during the Third Crusade. Besides suffering direct persecution, Jews were not allowed to work in the established trades and professions. They became merchants and moneylenders (usurers) instead, but even this would not satisfy the Christians. Indeed it infuriated the proud English barons to find themselves indebted to their inferiors. Thus Jews like Isaac and Rebecca became the victims of Christian discrimination and oppression, and often were driven back to Moslem lands (like Spain) for their own safety.

ROBIN HOOD AND HIS MERRY MEN

Bullfinch's "Age of Chivalry" tells of an actual Robin Hood, born at Locksley in 1160 of noble extraction. He was forced into a life outside the law and defied the king and his constables with great audacity for many years. He died at eighty-seven when a treacherous relative, the Prioress of Kirkley nunnery, allowed him to bleed to death. Whether he existed or not, at least one detail of Scott's character must be fiction. It was not until the battle of Crecy in 1346 that the longbow came into widespread use as an efficient and potent weapon of war; the skill that Scott gives to Locksley and his contemporaries is at least 150 years premature. The earliest of the *Robin Hood* **ballads** from which Scott drew his material dates from the fifteenth century, but most are considerably later. Today they are all available in Volume Five of Child's English and Scottish Popular Ballads.

BRIEF SUMMARY

Wilfred of Ivanhoe, a young Saxon knight, returns from the Third Crusade to an England troubled by race hatred between Normans and Saxons. Misguided by the prejudices created by this conflict,

Ivanhoe's father, Cedric, forbade him to follow the Norman King Richard to the Holy Wars. When the boy disobeyed, Cedric disowned his only son. Now, disguised as a pilgrim, Ivanhoe makes his way to Ashby where he hopes to regain his father's favor and the hand of Rowena, Cedric's beautiful ward, by winning the great tournament there. On the way, a Norman crusader, Brian de Bois-Guilbert (the Templar) and his companion, Prior Aymer, ask the pilgrim to guide their party to Cedric's hall. Unaware that they intend to sample Rowena's legendary charms, the pilgrim agrees. Cedric welcomes the travelers warmly and hospitably until the Templar's attentions to Rowena become embarrassing. The Norman and the old Saxon trade slurs, and the pilgrim, unrecognized in his own home, challenges the Templar for the "absent" Ivanhoe. The disguised knight lingers overnight and saves a wayfaring Jewish merchant (whose race is detestable to both Norman and Saxon) from Bois-Guilbert's cutthroats. The Jew, Isaac of York, rewards him with the horse and armor he will need for the jousting at Ashby.

The day of the tournament arrives. Prince John presides over the festival in place of his brother, Richard the Lion-hearted. (Richard is known to have been taken prisoner by a former ally white returning home from the Crusade. In his absence, John plots to make himself king.) The Norman Prince insults Cedric, who has come hoping for a Saxon victory. As Bois-Guilbert and four Norman knights defeat one after another of their challengers, John gloats over the impending humiliation of the Saxon dogs. But when all seems lost, a single champion appears, identified only by the emblem "Desdichado," or "Disinherited." Isaac and his daughter, Rebecca, are among the crowd that wishes him well. He beats all five Normans in succession and names the Saxon beauty, Rowena, Queen of the Tournament (the privilege of the victor). He wins the next day's competition as well, with the aid of another anonymous knight, the powerful Black Sluggard. When he finally faints from the wounds of battle, his helmet is removed to reveal the face of Ivanhoe. Prince John's defeat is sealed by a Saxon marksman, Locksley, who outshoots John's choice in the archery contest.

As the tournament ends, De Bracy, one of John's lieutenants, conceives a passion for Rowena. With Bois-Guilbert as his accomplice, he abducts her along with Cedric's entire train in the forest. Among the prisoners are Isaac, Rebecca, and an unidentified sick man, whom Cedric rescued when their own train was stranded. De Bracy takes them all to Torquilstone, the castle of a sympathetic Norman baron, Front-de-Boeuf. Only two of Cedric's slaves, Gurth and Wamba, escape the ambush. But before long they are joined by Locksley (Robin Hood) and his forest outlaws, and later the Black Sluggard, in the attempt to liberate their master.

Cedric escapes from the castle through Wamba's self-sacrifice, but they must fight to free the rest. As the assault on the castle begins, Rebecca relays an account of the action to the wounded man she has been nursing since the tournament. Few besides his gentle nurse know that Ivanhoe is in the castle, and in their long hours together she has come to love him. With the help of a mad Saxon hag, Ulrica, who sets fire to the castle, the attack is successful. The Black Sluggard has mortally wounded Front-de Boeuf and captured De Bracy, but Bois-Guilbert escapes at the last moment with Rebecca. Rowena and the other prisoners are freed, but Athelstane, the only living heir to the Saxon royal line, loses his life attempting to stop Bois-Guilbert. After a brief rest and a grateful farewell to their gallant rescuers, Cedric and Rowena depart with Athelstane's funeral train. Isaac, released because of an old favor he and Rebecca have done Locksley, hurries to Templestowe (where Bois-Guilbert is believed to have fled) to ransom his daughter.

Rebecca, meanwhile, has been spared Bois-Guilbert's outrages by being jailed as a witch. Her abduction to the Templar stronghold, the Preceptory of Templestowe, coincides with the visit of the fanatical Grand Master of the Order, Beaumanoir, who sees witchcraft in Rebecca's held over Bois-Guilbert. Isaac is unable to ransom her, however, and she escapes immediate execution after her trial only by demanding a champion to prove her innocence. She desperately chooses Wilfred of Ivanhoe, who interrupts a reconciliation with his father to rush to her defense. His opponent is Bois-Guilbert himself. The match seems an uneven one, since the hard journey to Templestowe has aggravated Ivanhoe's wounds and fatigued him. But on the first pass Bois-Guilbert drops from his saddle untouched, dead of the "violence of his own conflicting passions." The Black Sluggard (now known to be King Richard) appears at this instant to censure the Templars. Athelstane, miraculously recovered from the dead, surrenders the Saxon title to the throne and swears to support Richard's reign. John's conspiracy to dethrone his brother is crushed, and for the first time Saxon and Norman come together behind a single English monarch.

Athelstane also gives up his claim to Rowena (an obstacle to her romance with Ivanhoe) and she is married to Ivanhoe with Cedric's full consent. Rebecca visits Rowena a few days later to thank her for her husband's gallantry and to behold the face he loves. She and Isaac leave England for Spain, a more tolerant country, where she will devote her life to comforting the sick and helpless. Despite the forecast of disaster for King Richard and an abrupt end to Ivanhoe's career in his service, the book ends in peace and joy.

DEDICATORY EPISTLE

In 1814 novels were considered unworthy of the genius of the most serious writers. When Scott, as one of England's foremost poets, turned to fiction in that year, therefore, he attempted to conceal the fact until his success was firmly established. *Waverley*, the first of his novels, was written anonymously, and Scott signed those that followed it "By the Author of Waverley." Since *Ivanhoe* (1819), the tenth of the Waverley series, was to be his first departure from native Scottish themes, however, he decided to invent a new name for the title page of this work. "Laurence Templeton," a suitably English-sounding but fictitious antiquary (student of the past), was his selection. And although his publishers insisted on the usual pseudonym, this name did appear under the Dedicatory Epistle of the first edition of *Ivanhoe*. The epistle dedicates the novel to another "more grave antiquary," Rev. Dr. Jonas Dryasdust. Templeton has chosen him for this honor partly on the strength of his Essays upon the Horn of King Ulphus, which reveal their common interest in "our Saxon forefathers." The honor may be a dubious one from the Reverend's point of view, however, for he has always regarded productions of this kind along with "the idle novels and romances of the day." In this letter of dedication, Templeton undertakes to persuade his old friend that his long-standing contempt for such work does not apply to the present book in which his name has been immortalized. Historical novels, the Reverend has said, require only as much skill as is needed to choose and piece together the remnants of the past in chronological order. Templeton's answer occupies the remainder of the letter, and consists in a discussion of the problems and difficulties a writer of historical romances must confront.

Why shouldn't England's past be as interesting to the public as Scotland's?, Templeton asks. The Reverend has had two explanations for this. First, the Scottish "past" (i.e. the time prior to their civilization and stabilization as a nation after the Jacobite rebellion in 1745) is barely two generations dead. In writing of that "past" the novelist may use personalities and events which many of his readers have known through their own acquaintance or through the accounts of an eyewitness. Moreover he has no difficulty in finding "all those minute circumstances belonging to private life and domestic character, all that gives verisimilitude to a narrative and individuality to the person introduced." But the English novelist has only the "dry, sapless, mouldering, and disjointed bones" of a past far beyond the reach of living men's memories out of which to construct his story. A second difficulty the Reverend sees is that the English reader is prejudiced against novels about his country's rude, unrefined, violent past, because his own life bears so little resemblance to this description. Templeton answers the first by observing that, however scanty the materials may be, a good antiquarian can discover enough about the past to reconstruct the private lives of his ancestors. And he believes that "the good nature and good sense" of an English reader will outweigh any prejudice in the appraisal of a work about the English past.

As to the fitness of an antiquary to the task of fiction. Templeton believes himself well-supplied with precedents who have succeeded at both occupations. A graver objection is that by "intermingling fiction with truth" he may misrepresent the past - the question of historical accuracy. A novel set in the distant past cannot be both popular with modern readers and faithful to history. (He cites one example of a popular work, Galland's *Arabian Nights*, which took liberties with historical fact; and one of an accurate book, Strutt's Queenhoo Hall, which failed to win an audience.) How free may a novelist be with the facts? In language, sentiments, and manners the same rules apply: emphasize the common ground of past and present, and embellish this with the peculiar characteristics of the past. The novelist must use his knowledge of human nature and assume that it has not changed since the time of which he writes. This will give him the materials of character and emotion. On the other hand, "the character and costume of the age must remain inviolate." As for language, it "must not be exclusively obsolete and unintelligible," but neither should it contain exclusively modern terms and constructions. Although he has tried to follow these principles, Templeton does not pretend to complete historical consistency: "It is extremely probable that I may have confused the manners of two or three centuries." But most readers are not historians and their enjoyment of the novel will not suffer from such inadvertent liberties. Historians, seeing the difficulty of his undertaking, will deal charitably with him.

Templeton reveals that his source for the events of the novel was the *Wardour Manuscript* (ranking in importance with the Bannatyne MS and the Auchinleck MS). The letter ends with a few personal notes and an invitation for Dryasdust to join him in wishing the worst for a vandal who destroyed a precious archaeological relic simply because it drew crowds that destroyed his grass. (Note here, in the footnote on improving the mailcoaches, and elsewhere throughout the letter, Scott's gentle ridicule of antiquarians. He loved the past himself, and he was therefore all the more conscious of the extremes and absurdities to which his hobby could lead.)

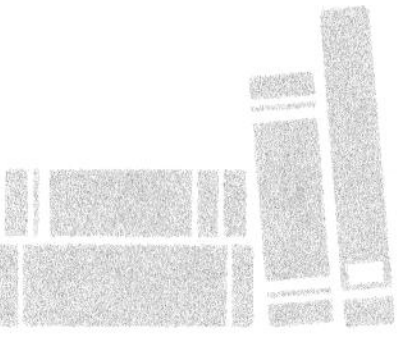

IVANHOE

TEXTUAL ANALYSIS

CHAPTERS 1-5

CHAPTER ONE

When Richard-the-Lion-Hearted ruled England, the great barons freely plundered the country and schemed to take the power of the crown into their own hands. Their ambitions depended upon two otherwise unrelated facts. First, the king who might have restrained them had been imprisoned in Austria while returning from the First Crusade (see Introduction). Few Englishmen expected he would live to reclaim the throne. Second, the country was divided between two proud and stubborn races: the Normans and the Saxons. The Saxons were the native inhabitants of the country; the Normans were descendants of the great Norman Duke, William the Conqueror, who had invaded England, defeated the Saxon army at Hastings (1066 A.D.), and occupied the land under Norman rule. Despite the passing of more than a century since that famous battle, the two races continued to live apart. The Norman aristocrats looked down upon the people they had beaten in war, continued to speak their native French, and practiced only French customs. They passed laws for their advantage and thwarted every attempt at Saxon recovery. Many Saxons yielded to these pressures and rejected their nationality. Others resisted with deepening pride in being Saxon and cherished any opportunity to prove that the better race had lost. But this antagonism suited the Norman barons perfectly, for they fed on the divisions and weakness of their enemies. With a helpless victim to exploit and no strong king to interfere, their prospects for success seemed brighter than ever before.

At sunset one day in a forest between Sheffield and York (in central England) two slaves of Cedric of Rotherwood, a prosperous Saxon thane (titled landowner), were driving some of their master's swine back home. The swineherd, a sullen fellow named Gurth, could scarcely keep the herd together without the help of his dog. Fangs. But the gamekeeper of a nearby Norman estate had disabled Fangs earlier in the day when he caught the dog trespassing on his master's property. Now, despite his willingness to obey, he could only limp in response to Gurth's commands. Wamba, a jester who accompanied Gurth, had no taste for heavy work and preferred to play with words. He observed that men used the Saxon words for meat animals (swine, ox, calf) as long as they were on the hoof and required human beings to tend them. But when the toil was done and the animals were cooked and ready to give pleasure, only Norman words would do (pork, beef, veal). The jest struck home to Gurth. He cursed the Norman tyranny and the injustice that Wamba's words had recalled to him. But an evening storm threatening in the distance halted the conversation. And even the sound of approaching hoofbeats could not distract Gurth any longer from his task.

Comment

The opening chapter has two primary functions. It provides us with all the historical background we will need to understand the beginning of the story; and, by introducing Gurth, it prepares us for one of the main conflicts of the novel: the racial struggle between Norman and Saxon. As Shakespeare often does, Scott begins his story with a dialogue between humble men who do not figure significantly in the plot, but whose conversation somehow prepares us for what is to follow. Wamba, furthermore, resembles the fool in *King Lear* in both the sharpness and the pertinence of his wit. His jest summarizes the Saxon condition better than Gurth's outbursts of indignation and rage.

The chapter begins with an epigraph (introductory quotation) from Homer's *Odyssey* and ends with a reference to Gurth as "this second Eumaeus." (Eumaeus is a swineherd in *The Odyssey*.) Scott's debt to Homer does not end there, however. Scott was not afraid to imitate what had been done well in the past, and we shall see later how the example of Homer shaped many of Scott's ideas about storytelling.

Scott is renowned for his "sense of the past" - his ability to establish the proper historical distance between his readers and the past of which he writes. Men and manners change over the centuries and Scott never lets us forget it. As early as paragraph one he stresses "the ancient times" in which his characters lived. He puts them in a forest with fabulous dragons and likens them to the heroes of old English ballads. This is not the harsh, blackened image of a great nation in the toils of industrial revolution - the England Scott and his audience knew; it is the "pleasant ... merry England" of long, long ago. The description of the glade in which Gurth and Wamba converse raises associations with the Roman occupation of Britain and, even further back, the Druids (ancient Celtic priests). And in the stiff dialogue and elaborate descriptions of dress (this book has been called a great "costumer novel") Scott is aiming, in part, to remark the strangeness of men materially different from us.

Antiquarians like Scott take particular delight in the resources of language. Wamba's jest is the best example in the first chapter, but more subtle are the names of the Norman barons: Front-de-Boeuf (bull's head) and Malvoisin (bad neighbor), both apparently chosen with ironical intent.

Note, finally, the occasional use of landscape description to underscore the action: the single large stone that opposes the flood Cedric), and the sobbing oaks that prophesy a storm. But, unlike the major Romantic poets, Scott considered no rural scene complete without human beings to populate it. He enjoyed nature, but never independently of human life.

CHAPTER TWO

Ten horsemen soon overtook the herd and its keepers. At their head rode two remarkable Normans: a pleasure-loving, worldly monk named Aymer, Prior of Jourvaulx Abbey; and a dark, powerful knight clad in mail and covered with a clerical tunic (we later learn that this is the uniform of the Knights-Templar). These were attended by two fierce Orientals, dark of skin and richly attired, followed in turn by a train of lesser churchmen. Prior Aymer's vices (specifically, drinking and hunting) had won him more local fame than censure. Among the wealthy Normans he amused the ladies, hunted with the men, and awed the elderly with "his supposed learning." The common people were satisfied with him for a somewhat different reason: "He was generous; and charity, as it is well known, covereth a multitude of sins, in another sense than that in which it is said to do so in Scriptures." Gurth and Wamba thus had no difficulty recognizing Aymer as he rode up to them. He asked the way to the hall of Cedric the Saxon, where he and his company intended to settle for the night. In this ancient time, such clergymen were often as prosperous as the aristocrats they served. As Cedric's serfs, therefore, Gurth and Wamba questioned the justice of the Prior's demand for hospitality that he was well able to pay for. Unruffled, Aymer replied that it was a priest's duty to provide others with an opportunity for charity. But the other horseman (the Templar) was not so patient with the insolence of Saxon peasants. He attempted to force a civil answer out of them at the point of a lance. Aymer knew their temperament somewhat better and restrained the Templar long enough to bribe Wamba with a gold coin; but the damage was done. The fool coolly marked out a course that passed far from Cedric's door, and sent them away confident that they had won their point.

The monk and the Templar rode on and resumed their conversation. The topic was dear to both: the beauty of women. And the particular lady under discussion was Rowena, ward of Cedric the Saxon. The Templar had never seen the lady but he was skeptical of the Prior's extravagant claims for her beauty. He wagered "ten butts of Chian wine" that he had seen her equal within the last year. Although happy to prove his point and win the wager, Aymer cautioned his hot-tempered friend against angering Cedric, who reportedly "banished his only son from his family for lifting his eyes in the way of affection towards this beauty." Fortunately for the Normans, this talk and their faulty recollection of Wamba's misdirections required them to ask the help of yet another wayfarer. This time their guide was a Palmer (pilgrim) whom they found sleeping at the foot of a sunken cross. His intimate knowledge of the country, despite a long absence in the Holy Land, led them all at last to Cedric's stronghold. By now the storm had begun, and the Templar blew his horn loudly to announce their arrival.

Comment

Again the epigraph reveals both a debt and a prominent **theme** in the chapter. The debt is to Chaucer for the characterization of the medieval monk more concerned for his sports and appetites than for the souls of his congregation. Aymer gambles and appraises women with the skill of a playboy. The **theme** is the division between the privileged Normans and the downtrodden Saxons even in matters of religion. Scott has prepared us for political and economic evils in Chapter I, but the hypocritical attitude of this worldly Norman priest is more than we might have expected. Even honest spiritual guidance is denied the poor Saxon.

Scott is no religious reformer, however, and he describes this outrage merely as another illustration of Saxon hardship. Indeed, Scott enjoys caricaturing the clergy too much to be offended at their corruption. He lived and died a Protestant, but he was never a militant one. Aymer and the Friar of Copmanhurst (Friar Tuck), whom we shall meet later, are drawn to entertain and not to infuriate us. This gentle ridicule and even the more vigorous attack upon the Templars are the least one might expect of a respectable English Protestant writing about medieval Catholicism.

Fascinated as Scott obviously is with this monk, Aymer is not the most important figure in the chapter. For when Scott introduces a character without naming him there is good cause to be on our guard. Mysterious strangers abound in Scott's novels, and in this chapter we meet two of them. The first is the unidentified Knight-Templar, a fierce and passionate (note this especially) Norman champion just returned from the Crusades. His clothing and expression are fully described, but his identity is curiously withheld from us. The second, the Palmer who arouses our suspicions by his familiarity with Cedric's property, is deliberately made inconspicuous by the absence of any attempt to describe him. In a novel overloaded with long and detailed descriptions of everything from costumes to castles, such an omission can scarcely be accidental, as we shall see presently.

Just as the first chapter has shown us a pair of contrasting Saxon types, the second produces an equally contrasting pair of Normans. Already in this scene the attitudes and temperaments that will divide the major actors in the novel are apparent. Aymer with some justice describes the Saxons as a "savage, fierce, intractable race," and Cedric the Saxon in particular as "proud, fierce, jealous, and irritable." Gurth and Wamba, speaking for the Saxon point of view, are less well-spoken, but equally sensitive to the monstrous faults of their oppressors.

Scott never capitalized upon the fashion of the exotic in the way that Byron did. But neither did he pass up this natural opportunity to sketch a couple of mysterious Orientals into his canvas. The Templar's Saracen slaves are thin stereotypes, but the strange luxuriousness of their clothing and the evil in their mute, somber faces appealed to Scott and almost certainly to the audience that made Byron's mediocre Oriental tales the popular success of the age.

The idea that facial expressions and features mirror a man's mind and spirit is older than Plato, who was its most famous exponent. For him and countless other thinkers, character is written all over a man's face: an evil man is likely to be ugly, a good one beautiful. A natural extension of this is that creators of fiction - dramatists, novelists, poets - often draw characters with this standard in mind. Homer's famous description of the rebel Thersites in the *Iliad* is probably the earliest instance of this sort of characterization in Western literature; Spenser's dragons, Shakespeare's villains (e.g., Aaron in *Titus Andronicus*), Milton's Satan, and Swift's Yahoos are examples in English literature. This is no place to dwell upon the different ways great authors of the past have chosen to express the reflection of the spiritual in the physical; what is significant is Scott's version of this principle. For him, as for Shakespeare in *Titus*, the condition of the soul is rendered in the color of the face and hair. It is generally true that the "dark heroes" of Scott's novels are either villains or moral defectives. For the most part they are brooding, passionate, Satanic men, and their common emblem is black hair and a dark complexion. (See Welsh, *Hero of the Waverley Novels*, for modifications and a complete list of such characters.) Among these dark heroes, one of the darkest is surely the Templar. His features "had been burnt almost into Negro blackness" and were surmounted by "thick curled hair of a raven blackness" (Chapter IV.) His passionate nature is apparent in "thick black moustaches [which] quivered upon the slightest emotion." And "his keen, piercing, dark eyes" are plainly those of a man who delights in having his will. As his character develops, we shall see how fully the dark promise of Bois-Guilbert's face is met.

CHAPTER THREE

Inside the rude Saxon hall, Cedric sat impatiently among his dogs, He was angered and concerned at the absence of both Rowena and his serfs, Gurth and Wamba, from the evening meal. He feared the worst for Gurth and the herd (by now long overdue), for it was common for outlaws and high-handed barons to prey upon Saxon property. Wamba's gaiety and impudence were missed in the gloom of the nearly empty hall. Rowena was busy changing her clothes, which had been dampened by the storm on her return home from church. Hoping to comfort Cedric, a servant mentioned that the curfew bell (another token of Norman rule) had not rung so long ago as to give cause for alarm about Gurth. But far from being comforted the old man flew into a tirade against this law that "compels men to extinguish their lights, that thieves and robbers may work their deeds in darkness." He swore to avenge this and other injustices on the field of battle against these Norman churls despite his nearly sixty years. But the melancholy thought that his only son was not by his side to comfort and assist him tamed the outburst: "Ah, Wilfred, Wilfred!" he exclaimed in a lower tone, 'couldst thou have ruled thine unreasonable passions, thy father had not been left in his age like the solitary oak, that throws out its shattered and unprotected branches against the full sweep of the tempest!" (Note the echo of the storm-tossed oak in Chapter 1.)

This mood abruptly gave way to clamor and alarm when the sound of the Templar's horn broke upon the hall. But once informed of his visitors' identities and their request for food and shelter, Cedric ordered the best his modest estate could provide to uphold the fame of Saxon hospitality. He remembered the Prior as the brother of a Norman usurper and as "a free and jovial priest, who loves the wine-cup and the bugle horn (hunting) better than bell and book (religion)." Brian de Bois-Guilbert, for such was the Templar's name, brought with him a mixed reputation for good and evil: "the bravest of his order; but stained with their usual vices, pride, arrogance, cruelty, and voluptuousness; a hard-hearted man who knows neither fear of earth, nor awe of heaven." Because of the arrival of strange guests, Cedric excused the Lady Rowena from coming to the hall. But an impertinent servant reminded him that Rowena was not likely to miss an opportunity "to hear the latest news from Palestine." Once again a servant's words reminded Cedric of the son he had disowned, for Wilfred had disobediently joined the "dissolute crusaders" and "hypocritical pilgrims" who "rushed into excess and blood guiltiness, and called it an accomplishment of the will of God." But his reverie was broken by the entrance of his guests.

Comment

Cedric's hall is the first of the four main settings in the novel (Ashby, Tourquilstone, and Templestowe are the others), and it is described in considerable detail. A drafty, uncomfortable place, it has none of the refinements and conveniences that French dwellings could boast of. Cedric himself is a striking figure - powerful and vigorous, blue-eyed and yellow-haired (note the contrast to Bois-Guilbert). His sole purpose in life seems to be the perpetuation of Saxon civilization. Yet every word he speaks reflects his dread of the inevitable extinction of the way of life he cherishes.

Again the main subject of the chapter is the injuries Saxons suffer under the discriminatory laws of their conquerors. But this time we see the problem from the point of view of a Saxon thane. His herds have been stolen, his friends dispossessed, and he must endure a humiliating curfew. These thoughts naturally raise bitter memories of the son he had banished. And when Rowena's servant hints that the visitors may bring news of Wilfred, Cedric has all he can do to contain his delight at this unexpected good fortune. This conflict between past injuries and natural love for his son divides Cedric's heart for most of the novel. The precise reason why he banished his son is never entirely clear. Rumor has it that it was because of Wilfred's romance with Rowena, although later disclosures suggest that Cedric's motives were more political than jealous. Another motive, and perhaps a more fundamental one, is his disapproval of Wilfred's sympathy with the great crusade, which he regards as unholy and irresponsible. But these earlier differences are temporarily blurred by the happy prospect of news of the boy's welfare.

In order to keep the sequence of the action intact, Scott uses a favorite device, the sound of a horn, as a reference point for the reader. The last chapter ended with a blast on Bois-Guilbert's horn, but Scott will not have us walk uninitiated into Cedric's hall. He must first describe it, tell us about its tenants, and something of the mood of the place. Only then will he resume the action by repeating the same horn blast. Scott indulges his love of description and lengthy background for even minor characters (another Homeric technique) but it costs him a fast-moving, uninterrupted plot.

CHAPTER FOUR

The Prior and the Templar wore their richest robes to Cedric's table. Aymer decorated his fingers with jewels and groomed himself as fashionably as his holy order would permit. Bois-Guilbert's head was uncovered to reveal a mass of thick black hair which suited his "unusually swart complexion" well. He seemed more proud than ever as he strutted into the hall. As they and their train were seated, the Pilgrim, covered by a black cloak, passed unnoticed to the fireplace, Cedric welcomed them all politely, but within the limitations of his vow never to leave his platform to greet a Norman guest nor even to speak in the Norman-French language. Aymer returned the greeting in Saxon with great respect for his host's vows; but the Templar said simply, "I speak ever French, the language of King Richard and his nobles; but I understand English sufficiently to communicate with the natives of that country." Suppressing his displeasure at this reply, Cedric diverted his anger toward Gurth, who had only now entered the hall. His first impulse was to punish the laggardly serf, but Wamba explained that they had been delayed for the want of Fangs' help. Still eager for a scapegoat, Cedric reviled the dog; but again Wamba frustrated him. Fangs couldn't help because of the lameness that interfered with his work, Wamba insisted, and the lameness had come at the hands of a Norman gamekeeper, and not by any mischief on the dog's part. With no one else to blame, Cedric blustered and sputtered about the violations of his property by unscrupulous Norman barons.

Cedric spread an enormous feast for his guests. Just as dinner was to begin, the Lady Rowena appeared. The moment he saw her Bois-Guilbert conceded his wager to the good Prior: "I shall wear no gold collar of yours at the tournament. The Chian wine is your own." He could not take his eyes from her until Cedric, whose jealous concern for Rowena was common gossip, checked his boldness: "'Sir Templar,' said he, 'the cheeks of our Saxon maidens have seen too little of the sun to enable them to bear the fixed glance of a crusader.'" Even the Templar's apology concealed an insult to his host. But the tactful Prior was quick to turn the conversation to the coming tournament at Ashby-de-la-Zouche. Cedric had no use for these French "vanities," and rejected the Templar's offer to escort his party in the event that he should decide to attend. Athelstane of Coningsburgh, "my noble neighbor and countryman" (and, we later learn, direct heir to the defunct Saxon throne), would be company and protection enough. After dinner Cedric proposed a toast to the Prior, unless he should "be so rigid in adhering to monastic rule as to prefer [the sour milk his order prescribed]." But the thick-skinned Prior evaded the **irony** and drank the toast with "honest wine." Bois-Guilbert drank to Rowena, and she returned his courtesy with a request for the news from Palestine. He announced a recent truce with Saladin, the Saracen leader, but Wamba was cynical in response: "These truces . . . make an old man of me," he moaned, for each of the three he could remember "was to endure the course of fifty years; so that, by computation, I must be at least a hundred and fifty years old." This jest was costly, however, for it reminded the Templar that this same jackanapes had misguided his train earlier that evening. Only the report of yet another "stranger at the gate, imploring admittance and hospitality" saved Wamba from a sound thrashing. The generous Cedric deferred Wamba's punishment and commanded that this newcomer be granted the liberty of the house.

Comment

Here Scott begins to develop in detail the racial antagonism mentioned in the previous chapters. Despite Cedric's good intentions and the diplomacy of the Prior (who knows better than to bite a hand that is about to feed him), the hatred between the two races simmers beneath the surface of their polite conversation. Every civil word the Templar speaks harbors two more of contempt; and Cedric, always a correct and generous host, nevertheless manages to return every insult he sustains. Language again symbolizes the distance between Norman and Saxon. And the Templar's refusal to speak in Saxon makes him a partisan worthy to contend with the fanatical Cedric. Disregarding Aymer's advice, he brazenly enjoys the sight of Rowena's beauty; and when Cedric tells him to look away he complies, but without an apology suitable to the offense. By the end of the chapter feelings are running high on both sides, and the arrival of a stranger is a welcome relief.

Rowena, like most of Scott's heroines, is a stately, fair, blue-eyed beauty. She is gentle and pious, yet noble and independent enough to have her own way when she is determined. Her confrontation with the Templar borders on allegory. She embodies all the innocent, bright light of maiden virtue; and Bois-Guilbert assails her with the rude stare of an accomplished sensualist. It is a conflict between white and black, good and evil; and, as always in Scott, the power of darkness is defeated.

CHAPTER FIVE

The stranger was announced as Isaac of York, a Jew, and for a moment the enemies in the hall were united in displeasure at the approach of a heathen. Wamba, "with his usual effrontery," ridiculed the Jewish custom that prohibited eating of the flesh of pigs. First he recommended Gurth, the swineherd, as "a fit usher to the Jew." And when Cedric playfully threatened to seat the Jew with him ("the fool and the knave will be well met"), Wamba missed a side of bacon to protect himself. Prior Aymer hurriedly blessed himself, and the Templar defied the "dog Jew to approach a defender of the Holy Sepulchre." No less displeased than his guests, Cedric would yet deny his hospitality to no man, and ordered the Jew to be admitted. Isaac was a tall old man, who stooped from accustomed humility and fear in a land hostile to his race. For, "during those dark ages," the Jew "was alike detested by the credulous and prejudiced vulgar, and persecuted by the greedy and rapacious nobility." Cedric greeted him coldly and permitted him to seek a place at the lower table. But as he went down the aisle Isaac met only the "pious horror" of Aymer's attendants and the scowls of the Templar's "heathen Saracens." The pilgrim alone spoke to the frightened, hungry old man, offering him a place by the fire where he might dry his clothes and fill his stomach in peace. Cedric's attention had, by this time, been diverted to Aymer's talk about a common interest: hunting. But even this neutral subject raised the issue of racial pride. Aymer defended the use of French terms in the sport and Cedric was equally vehement in support of the English. The dispute soon ended as the Saxon sadly reminisced about a happier time when "the Saxon war-cry was . . . heard as far within the ranks of the Scottish host as the cri de guerre of the boldest Norman baron." With that Cedric raised his cup to "the best in Palestine among the champions of the Cross," regardless of race or language. The Templar promptly accepted the honor for his order, but Aymer spoke up for the Knights Hospitaller (his brother among them). As they disputed the Lady Rowena inquired how well the English warriors had borne themselves. His memory somewhat improved by her question, Bois-Guilbert granted that only the Templars were superior to Richard's English Knights. "'Second to None,' said the Pilgrim." For the first time since his appearance in the hall, the Pilgrim broke his silence. And with unexpected firmness he reminded the Templar of the day following the siege of Acre when King Richard and five of his knights had each defeated three challengers, including Bois-Guilbert himself and six other Templars. Cedric, oblivious to the rage on the darkened face of the Templar, eagerly asked who these worthy heroes were. One by one, beginning with Richard himself, the pilgrim named them. Cedric's excitement and anticipation grew as he heard the list, for his own son, Wilfred of Ivanhoe, had taken arms with Richard. His expectations seemed to be disappointed when the pilgrim could not recall the last knight's name. But the Templar remembered him well: "It was the Knight of Ivanhoe." Blaming his defeat at this boy's hands on a lame horse and bad fortune, Bois-Guilbert laid down a new challenge to the absent Ivanhoe that seemed unlikely to be accepted. But the Palmer would not let the Templar's boast pass and accepted the challenge in the young knight's name, should he ever return home. They angrily deposited the pledges of their agreement with Prior Aymer-a fragment of the true cross from the Palmer and a golden chain from the Templar. Rowena offered to put her reputation behind the Palmer's pledge; and Cedric, troubled by "a crowd of conflicting emotions . . . gratified pride, resentment, embarrassment," said he would willingly have made the pledge himself, had the Palmer not already done it so well. Once the pledges were safely away, the Prior ("a hater of all feuds and brawls") brought the evening to a close. He was afraid of trouble between the Saxon and the Templar, and not even Cedric's challenge to his reputation as a great drinker could shake this "professional peacemaker" from the sensible course he had chosen. The final cup was drained and the guests dispersed. As the Templar passed Isaac he demanded to know if he was bound for the tournament at Ashby and how much money he carried in his purse. He cursed him for being a usurer and, when the old Jew denied it, a liar as well. Passing on to his slaves, he spoke to them briefly in a strange tongue and then left the hall with the Prior and their company.

Comment

By now it is clear how deliberate Scott has been in the introduction of his characters. After pairs of Saxons and Normans, we meet, consecutively, the Palmer, Cedric, Rowena, and Isaac. Of these, only Cedric has held the stage alone, but in the manner of their appearance each has claimed our undivided attention. The actors are in place and the action may now begin.

Scott's delineation of Isaac and the condition of his people in Richard's England is a rare achievement. Isaac himself is something of a stereotype, with his submissive posture and his crooked nose; but Scott is not only aware of this-he justifies the kind of portrait he has drawn. Prejudice and hatred invent racial types and then compel their victims to live up to the type-to behave and look the way their persecutors expect. Far from overgeneralizing and blurring Isaac's character, therefore, Scott is recording the impression of a subtle and insidious social evil upon this man's face and bearing.

Indeed, the appearance of Isaac crystallizes for the first time a major **theme** of the novel that had only been hinted at before in the hatred between Norman and Saxon. The one characteristic that all of Ivanhoe's adversaries share is bigotry; we might almost say that bigotry itself - the irrational hatred of other human beings because of race or creed - is the antagonist in this novel. Isaac's reception in the great Saxon hall illustrates a number of variations on the **theme** of bigotry. Wamba's jesting about pork has its modern counterpart in religious jokes - both depending upon blind preconceptions and faulty generalizations about a minority for their humor. Aymer's superstitious horror of meeting a non-Christian is perhaps less common today, but the militant, aggressive hate of a man like Bois-Guilbert especially when it is aggravated by the frustration and defeat that he meets among equals is only too familiar. The supreme **irony** of the chapter is that the Prior and the Templar have expressed no qualms about sharing the road and the dinner table with a pair of bloodthirsty Saracens-sons of a nation dedicated to the slaughter of Christians and themselves once soldiers in that cause. That a harmless, hungry old man could raise such fears and bitterness in men untroubled by the constant company of Moslem cutthroats is a splendid illustration of the absurdity of racial prejudice.

The absence of a weapon on Isaac's person, the Templar's charge that he practices usury (money-lending), the mention of an Exchequer of Jews (a heavy tax), and the nearly universal scorn with which Isaac is met are wholly typical of the status of the Jew in England at this time. Scott makes clear that bigotry is a familiar enemy to Isaac. Even Cedric, although more humane than his Norman guests, regards the Jew with contempt. It is an idea that cuts across national boundaries and not even the noblest of characters in this novel is quite free of it.

Isaac is Scott's third explicit debt to an earlier and greater writer. He is a direct literary descendant of Shylock in Shakespeare's *The Merchant of Venice*, and Scott again acknowledges the debt by quoting that play in the epigraph. If Isaac lacks the cunning and articulateness of his model, he also lacks Shylock's unscrupulousness. Scott gives Isaac no opportunity to strike back at his persecutors, and thus he has neither vigor nor pride, and we must respect him less than Shylock. In short, Scott has not repeated Shakespeare's brilliant success, but Isaac remains a memorable and worthy addition to the illustrious gallery of Jewish characters in literature.

Besides introducing Isaac, this chapter reaches a **climax** in the growing feud between Cedric and Bois-Guilbert. The Templar's mood gradually deteriorates from insolent superiority to rage as Cedric's improves from melancholy to great joy. The exposure of Bois-Guilbert's false claims and the news of Ivanhoe, both accomplished by the Palmer's short, forceful speech, turn the evening in favor of the Saxons. Indeed the change occurs in the very sequence of the names of Richard's Knights. After the king, the Palmer names in turn a Norman, a Norman of Saxon descent, a Saxon (on his mother's side), and finally a "genuine Saxon." To save face, Bois-Guilbert adds the name of Ivanhoe and utters an empty challenge. But he fails even here to outdo the Palmer. Only Aymer's level-headedness spares the Templar (and his host) further embarrassment.

Despite his pivotal role, we learn little more about the Palmer. He was kind to Isaac, but what can his uncharacteristic lapse of memory in forgetting the name of Ivanhoe mean? Certainly he has come off well thus far, even in the pledge he offers. Aymer himself obviously prizes the sacred relic above the Templar's chain. One of two motives attracted brave men to the Holy Land (although Cedric recognizes only the first): greed and piety. And Scott has made it easy for us to distinguish the fortune-hunter from the man of God by the precious objects each presents to bind his pledge.

The significance of language as a symbol of national pride is again pointed up in this chapter. Scott has called our attention to it repeatedly, but this time the speaker is by his own admission the last guardian of a dying culture: "But our bards are no more, our deeds are lost in those of another race-our language-our very name is hastening to decay, and none mourns for it save one solitary old man." His battle is lost and the language will not survive him, but he will honor it stubbornly until the end. Scott was no friend of artificial barriers between related cultures; as a Scotsman in Great Britain he had good reason to hate them. But he also learned to love the vanishing dialects of the Scottish countryside-enough to have written them into the speeches of his most vivid characters. This affection for the old despite the knowledge that it must give way to new growth is a common sentiment in Scott's novels.

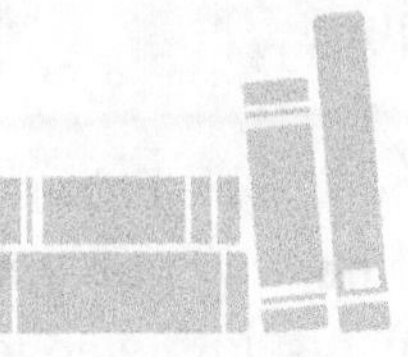

IVANHOE

TEXTUAL ANALYSIS

CHAPTERS 6–10

CHAPTER SIX

The Palmer was twice delayed on the way to his chamber. First Cedric's cupbearer, Oswald, appeared and offered him wine if he would come and tell some of the servants what else he knew of Ivanhoe's history. This invitation the Palmer declined, saying he had vowed "never to speak in the kitchen on matters which were prohibited in the hall." Disappointed and angered, Oswald ordered the Palmer to be taken to humbler quarters. He was not far along the new route, however, before a second servant stopped him. This time it was Rowena's waiting-maid with a message that her mistress wanted to speak with him. Without a word of opposition the Palmer followed her to Rowena's apartment. In that magnificent but comfortless room Rowena received him and asked after Ivanhoe. She had heard disturbing rumors of his illness in the Holy Land: that it had prevented his returning with the English army and exposed him to the "persecution of the French faction, to whom the Templars are known to be attached." The Palmer assured her that these dangers were over and he was now on his way home through France, aided there by his knowledge of the French tongue and French manners. But as to the time of Ivanhoe's return he could say nothing. Rowena was disappointed at this gap in the Palmer's information, for she dreaded the consequences of Ivanhoe's failure to arrive in time for the coming tournament. She feared especially that Athelstane-one of her own race-might win the prize (and possibly herself in the bargain). But as the Palmer could give her no further comfort, she thanked him with a piece of gold and allowed him to retire.

The new apartment that Oswald had assigned the Palmer was a tiny, bare cell with a straw bed and sheepskins for blankets. But he seemed satisfied because it was next to Gurth's quarters on the one side and the Jew's on the other. With no further ceremony he lay down fully clothed on the bed and rested there until dawn. When the sun arose the Palmer entered Isaac's chamber and awakened him from a fitful sleep. It was several moments before the Jew would believe that the good Palmer had neither stepped out of his nightmare nor come to harm him. He explained the purpose of his visit briefly. Isaac's life was in danger. Knowledge of the Saracen language had made it possible for him to overhear the Templar's command to his slaves the night before. They were told to abduct Isaac after he left the protection of Cedric's hall and to carry him to one of the neighboring Norman castles. Isaac fell at the Palmer's feet in terror at his news, but the holy man raised him with a promise to conduct him safely through Norman territory. Once out of danger, the Palmer went on, he could join "some chief or baron going to the tournament, whose good will you have probably the means of securing." This last phrase seemed to dampen the Jew's rising hopes of escape, for he blurted out that he had no money to buy a Christian's good will. Indeed he now feared that the Palmer expected to be rewarded as well. But the other disgustedly reminded Isaac that his religious vow bound him to a life of poverty. He freed the Jew to seek any other protection he might trust. But Isaac wisely saw that this holy man was his only ally in an alien land, and he now grew impatient for them to leave together.

In order to leave Cedric's hall without waking the other guests, the Palmer had to persuade Gurth to unlock the gates. The swineherd, sleepy and suspicious, refused to budge until the Palmer whispered a few Saxon words into his ear. Suddenly the sullen, uncooperative serf sprang into action, with a warning from the Palmer "to be prudent" about what he had heard. To the amazement of Isaac and Wamba, he opened the gates and fetched two mules to bear the fugitives away. Wamba, more accustomed to Gurth's stubborn ways, responded in the way he knew best-with a quip: "I wish I knew what you Palmer learn in the Holy Land." Before long Isaac and the Palmer were ready to leave. Isaac carefully tied a small blue bag to his saddle, mumbling that it carried only a change of clothes; and the Pilgrim received Gurth's kiss upon his hand before the two riders disappeared into the forest.

After a long and devious ride that brought them near the safety of the town of Sheffield, the Palmer drew up his horse. The time had come to part company, "for it beseems not men of my character and thine to travel together longer than needs must be." Nothing the Jew said could alter the Palmer's mind. But Isaac, nevertheless, saw fit to offer the Palmer a gift as a token of his gratitude. He had seen the chain and spurs of knighthood hidden beneath the Palmer's gown. Since this knight was obviously on his way to the tournament, Isaac reasoned that no gift could be more welcome than a horse and armor. Despite the great oppressions and taxes they suffered, the Jews in England had survived with "passive courage inspired by love of gain." Indeed, they "accumulated huge sums [of money] which they transferred . . . [by] bills of Exchange." It was by this method that Isaac arranged for his benefactor's reward. The Palmer accepted the note, but not before he had made some sport of the old man. First he teased Isaac about the money he probably carried in his bag. Then he warned the tight-fisted Jew that his gift would probably be lost and almost certainly damaged in the jousting. The Palmer smiled at the obvious conflict in Isaac's mind between gratitude and good business. But finally "his better feelings predominated over those which were most familiar to him." He insisted that the young knight accept the gift, adding hopefully, "Thrust thyself not too forward [in the lists, not for] the steed, and coat of armor, but for the sake of thine own life and limbs." As they parted, the Palmer promised the old man that he would restore the gift intact.

Comment

The mystery of the Palmer deepens in this chapter as he moves closer to the center of the action. His self-assurance and complete control of every situation he meets continue to impress us. His influence upon Gurth, in particular, surprises us as much as it does Wamba. What words could have transformed this proud, obstinate Saxon into an obliging, almost reverential servant of the Palmer's will? Even more astonishing is Isaac's discovery that the Palmer is a knight in disguise. This confirms any suspicions we may have had concerning his character and virtue, but Scott is still unwilling to satisfy our curiosity by naming him.

The Palmer betrays an almost aristocratic sense of good form in declining Oswald's invitation to speak to the servants.

Their secret interest in Ivanhoe's welfare, on the other hand, suggests that Cedric's banishment of the boy was probably an unpopular decision.

Two important disclosures emerge from the Palmer's interview with Rowena. First, Ivanhoe is returning from Palestine after an illness and some trouble with the Templars. Second, only his appearance and victory over Athelstane at Ashby can save him from "evil tidings" (Rowena's betrothal to another) when he returns. Thus Scott establishes both the nearness of Ivanhoe's homecoming and the need for it, and heightens our anticipation of that event.

Although ready enough to save a Jew's life, the Palmer is no different from others in the novel in his contempt for Isaac's race and amusement at his weaknesses. It is difficult to sort out Scott's attitudes from the Palmer's in the scene where Isaac reconsiders giving a gift to his rescuer. Scott's disapproval of race prejudice remains, but he lingers over Isaac's dilemma until it becomes comical. The pathetic image of the old man's fear-awakening from a nightmare, cringing and trembling before the man who came to save him-fades besides the folly of his greed. The frequency with which Scott exposes this moral blindness in Isaac very nearly deprives him of our sympathy at times.

CHAPTER SEVEN

Most Englishmen suffered greatly during King Richard's captivity. One cause for this suffering was the corrupt government that ruled the land in his absence. Prince John, Richard's own brother, plotted to keep him in the Duke of Austria's prison and to claim the throne when Richard did not re-appear. For this purpose, John gathered about him all the king's enemies he could find to help him rule the country: some feared the king's justice for crimes they committed in his absence; others returned from his crusade bitter and penniless, and ambitious for power and wealth. With such a government no Englishman was safe or free. Moreover, the land was pillaged by two kinds of outlaws. Some were foresters (yeomen) loyal to Richard, who found in thievery their only means of resisting the Norman barons. The others were the hired henchmen of the barons themselves, whose favorite prey were the helpless Saxons. The barons paid for these private armies by borrowing from Jewish usurers; and this debt ate deeply into Norman wealth, except when the baron chose to work "some act of unprincipled violence" upon his usurer. Finally, a nationwide epidemic of poverty and disease added to the hardships an Englishman had to face.

Despite these evils there was time for amusement and sport. The tournament was "the grand spectacle of that age" and attracted excited mobs of rich and poor alike, much like present-day bullfights in Spain. The "Passage of Arms" at Ashby, presided over by the Prince and matching the finest champions in the land, was one of the most famous of these events. So great was the crowd on the day of Ashby that there were frequent disputes among spectators for places suitable to their rank. Among the high-born such disputes were quickly settled by the officials, and soon the galleries were filled with noblemen and their ladies (although one would have thought the sport "too bloody and dangerous to afford their sex much pleasure"). But in the spaces between the lists and the galleries where the middle classes were crowded together it was no simple matter to keep the peace. One quarrel centered on "our acquaintance Isaac," whose recent business dealings with the Prince had given him some confidence among John's subjects. He had jostled a Norman "whose threadbare tunic bore witness to his poverty, as his sword, and dagger, and golden chain intimated his pretension to rank." A bystander - a "stout well-set yeoman" - warned Isaac to keep his place or lose his skin. But just as Isaac was about to back down, the crowd's attention was drawn to the entrance of the Prince and his company. Prior Aymer was with him, dressed as colorfully as ever; and the rest were all leaders of his hired armies and of the sympathetic Knights Templar and Knights of St. John. Prince John rode boldly into the arena, splendidly attired. His face showed "dissolute audacity, mingled with extreme haughtiness and indifference to the feelings of others." But most of the spectators mistook this for "manly frankness," and he entered amid "clamorous applause." As he circled the grounds John noticed the commotion that had arisen about Isaac. He noticed, too, the darkly beautiful girl who clung to the Jew's arm. This was Rebecca, Isaac's daughter, whose black hair, excellent features, and lovely neck and bosom made her a match for any of the English beauties present. John determined to make a place for this unpopular couple in the gallery above the crowd. As he searched for an empty place, his eye fell upon Athelstane who, with Cedric the Saxon and his party, was seated directly above the dispute. For all his size and strength, Athelstane was slow to act (he was nicknamed "Athelstane the Unready"), and when John ordered one of his knights (De Bracy) to move the sluggish Saxon aside to make way for Isaac, it was Cedric who swiftly drew his sword and cut the threatening lance in half. The general applause that greeted Cedric's intervention discouraged John from punishing the Saxon. Instead the Prince turned on a yeoman (the one who had warned Isaac) who seemed especially pleased at the Saxon's courage. Why did he cheer the Saxon? Because I like to see "a good shot or a gallant blow," he replied. And when John dared him to back this up in the archery contest, the yeoman coolly agreed to try his skill. By now the angry Prince would tolerate no further delay. Over Isaac's feeble objections John ordered him to take a place among Cedric's party. But this time Wamba's timely action averted disaster. Answering the king's dare to anyone who would stop the Jew, Wamba rushed up to the old man as he slowly mounted the stairs and thrust "a shield of brawn" (bacon) into his beard. At the same time he drew his wooden sword and swung it over his head as if to punish a knight in the lists. Isaac started back, slipped, and tumbled down the stairs to the delight of the spectators. Even the Prince could not help laughing at the jest. In keeping with the mockery Wamba had begun, John agreed that the victor should not sit with his victim. He ordered Isaac to a better place in the area to which he had just returned. Far from punishing the fool who had thwarted him, John snatched away Isaac's purse and threw a couple of golden coins from it to the author of such a fine prank. And amid the applause and delight of his audience, the Prince left the scene of Isaac's humiliation to finish his parade about the lists.

Comment

The tournament at Ashby shows Scott at his most picturesque. From the "singularly romantic" setting of the arena to the gorgeous costumes of the contestants, he glories in the color and the pageantry of England in the age of chivalry. But he does not allow the spectacle to hide the poverty and coarseness beneath its surface. He notes in passing to ladies' unfeminine enthusiasm for blood-letting; the analogy to Spanish bullfights is a biting comment on the cruelty of such entertainment. Cynicism tinged with **irony** does not become the dominant tone until Chapter XII. But even in the portrait of the sinister Prince John we can see unreality of appearances - the illusion of the scene. A man with corruption and decadence written plainly across his face, John is yet a favorite with the crowd because of his horsemanship, fancy clothing, and grand gestures.

Along with Prince John, we meet a number of other secondary characters in this chapter. De Bracy, Front-de-Boeuf, Athelstane, and the Yeoman (drawn, like Prior Aymer, from Chaucer) will all figure prominently in later chapters, but are introduced rather quietly here. Less subtle is the debut of Rebecca, who is described with great care and affection. Unlike Rowena, she is dark-haired and somewhat exotic in dress and features; nor is she so careful to conceal her charms as Rowena. Despite the lavish description, however, she does nothing of importance in this chapter.

Like Cedric's hall, Ashby is a crossroads for the principals in the action and Scott is careful to develop it as a major setting of the novel. Isaac's appearance in the crowd might have been expected; but Cedric had not intended to come. Athelstane's ponderous presence reminds us of Rowena's wish that Ivanhoe might return in time to prevent him from winning the prize. And with Bois-Guilbert occupying the central challenger's tent, the only notable absentees are the Palmer and Ivanhoe himself.

The tournament also offers Scott a unique opportunity for describing the general conditions of the English nation at this time. Because of the natural segregation of classes at the lists, the tournament is a scale model of medieval English society. The nobility sits comfortably in the galleries, the lower classes stretch their necks outside the arena, and the middle class is squeezed tightly between the galleries and the lists. Naturally enough, therefore, Scott begins the chapter with a broad survey of political and social afflictions in the land. But only three of the details he mentions prepare us to understand the rest of the novel: 1) John's plot to usurp Richard's throne, 2) the existence of outlaw bands of yeomen (which Scott strives to justify), and 3) the nobles who employ private armies to protect their castles and territory.

CHAPTER EIGHT

Midway through his entrance Prince John remembered that he had yet to name a Queen of Love and Beauty to preside over the tournament opposite him. The exquisite Rebecca was fresh in him memory, so he told Prior Aymer that he would choose her for the honor. The monk was astounded at the thought of a Jewess for a Queen, and recommended Rowena as a more suitable choice. But the motive for John's decision lay deeper than Rebecca's beauty. He would prefer a Jewess to Rowena "were it only to mortify the Saxon churls." Aymer's objections were seconded, however, by De Bracy and Waldemar Fitzurse (John's closest supporter and adviser), who warned that such vindictiveness was bound to lead to trouble. De Bracy proposed an unusual but fair solution to the problem: let the conqueror of the day name the Queen. Reluctantly the Prince agreed, seeing the folly of losing his supporters over a trifle. This formality out of the way, a herald read the laws of the tournament. Then, from among a crowd of worthy knights (called "champions"), five entered through the north portal to challenge the strongest lances in England (called "challengers" and led by Brian de Bois-Guilbert and his fellow Templar, Reginald Front-de-Boeuf). Although the names of these champions have been erased from memory, on this day they held the attention of a multitude of spectators. They approached the challengers' tents at the south end of the lists and each touched the shield of his chosen opponent with the dull end of his lance (indicating an invitation to combat using only blunted lances). The challengers emerged and took their places opposite their adversaries. The trumpets blared and the favorites bore three men solidly to the ground and bested the other two. Two more sets of challengers went as quickly to defeat. By the fourth round only three knights came forward to meet the challengers. After these, too, were beaten, no one appeared willing to renew the fighting. During the long pause that followed, Cedric asked Athelstane to make some attempt to salvage the honor of England from what otherwise seemed a certain victory for the Norman side. But his reply did little to satisfy the old Saxon: "I shall tilt tomorrow in the melee; it is not worthwhile for me to arm myself today." Both the spirit and the letter of these words irritated Cedric: the spirit, because Athelstane did not hold his country's honor above his own; the letter, in his thoughtless use of a Norman word. So indifferent and dull was Athelstane that he accepted Wamba's insulting jest as a compliment ("It was better, though scarce easier, to be the best man among a hundred, than the best man of two.") As time passed and no trumpet answered the boastful music of the challengers, there seemed no alternative but to award Bois-Guilbert the prize. Old men grumbled at the decay of chivalry and Saxons stewed silently in their embarrassment. But when everything seemed over, "a solitary trumpet which breathed a note of defiance" revived the crowd's hope. A single knight appeared in magnificent armor that bore the emblem of "a young oak-tree pulled up by the roots, with the Spanish word Desdichado signifying Disinherited." His horsemanship and gallantry immediately won the crowd over, and the common people advised him which opponent would give him the easiest ride to the dirt. But despite their good intentions, the knight rode directly up to Bois-Guilbert's shield and touched it with the point of his lance! (Signifying mortal combat with real weapons.) The Templar was as amazed as the rest and chided the newcomer. Had he had the sacraments of the church on this last day of his life? But for all his cockiness the Templar was careful to change to a fresh horse and better armor. Their first pass was fierce but inconclusive; but on the second the Disinherited Knight unhorsed the Templar with a skillful maneuver and gained the first victory of the day over the challengers. Bois-Guilbert angrily drew his sword and went for his young conqueror when he arose from the dirt, and as the marshals forced them apart (swordplay was forbidden) they exchanged a challenge to fight some day without interference. During a brief lull the winner drank a toast "To all true English hearts, and to the confusion of foreign tyrants." And before long he was back to take on the rest, led by "the gigantic Front-de-Boeuf." With extraordinary courage and courtesy the anonymous knight gained the advantage over all four. Amid unanimous acclaim the Disinherited Knight was awarded the prize and the right to name the Queen of Love and Beauty.

Comment

It should not be necessary to apologize for the obvious melodrama of this chapter. In a story of adventure and heroic exploit nothing is more appropriate than the last-second entrance of a single hero, who turns back a seemingly invincible enemy (or several of them, as the case may be). It is improbable, unrealistic, and artificial but it is also the stock-in-trade of all great storytellers from Homer to the present.

During the last chapter it became clear that Scott was moving his cast of characters into place at Ashby for good reason. He had already established conflicts between Norman and Saxon, Jew and Gentile, and aroused our curiosity about the Palmer and our expectations of Ivanhoe's arrival. Now he allows the Templar and his comrades to cut down the flower of English knighthood and to come within a hair's breadth of winning the day's honors. Having pushed the suspense as far as he could, Scott must now produce a hero. Every circumstance of the plot demands it, and Scott rarely disappoints his readers. Whether he is the Palmer, Ivanhoe, or King Richard himself, the Disinherited Knight predictably appears to save the day.

As in Homer, the emblem on a warrior's shield is of great significance to Scott. Bois-Guilbert's emblem-a ravenous black bird of prey-corresponds closely to his character and the policies of his order in terrorizing the English common people. The uprooted oak and the word "disinherited" or "disenchanted," have likewise great appropriateness, as we shall see.

CHAPTER NINE

Only after his victories did the identity of the Disinherited Knight begin to interest the spectators. Anonymity at a tournament was common in these chivalrous times, but it was inevitable that so staunch a fighter should excite curiosity. No one was more curious than Prince John, who asked the members of his party their opinion in the mystery. The question drew no response but for their common expression of admiration for the knight's skill - not, at least, until Fitzurse guessed that he might "be one of the good lances who accompanied King Richard to Palestine, and who are now struggling homeward from the Holy Land." This speculation set off a chain of others, until John was very nearly convinced that he had seen none other than Richard the Lion-Hearted himself in action that day. His terror was evident, despite Fitzurse's sensible reminder that the champion before them was far inferior to the king both in size and weight. Nevertheless John delivered the prize-a magnificent charger - which the knight silently accepted. He mounted the beast and cantered twice around the lists to display him. Only one formality remained: the selection of a Queen. The conqueror was to deliver the symbolic coronet of honor to the lady of his choice, thus designating her the Queen of Love and Beauty over the next day's combat. Content that this was not the king, John recalled the Disinherited Knight to him and placed the coronet on the point of his lance. At the same time he hinted broadly that it would be difficult to choose any one but Alicia, daughter of Waldemar Fitzurse. The wily Prince hoped by this strategy to blot out the memory of his unpopular nomination of Rebecca earlier in the day. But he also saw some profit in setting the Disinherited Knight and Fitzurse at odds, should the knight honor another lady. After carefully inspecting the many Norman beauties in the crowd the Disinherited Knight reached Cedric's balcony - a section that had applauded his courage with exceptional enthusiasm. Just below them Isaac the Jew had also watched with more than common concern. Indeed, by his familiarity with the knight's horse and armor, it seemed almost as if Isaac alone among the multitude knew the secret of his identity. Rebecca had tried vainly to correct her father's fears for the armor. And as the challengers began to fall, Isaac kept busy calculating the knight's profit from the armor that his victims thereby forfeited to him. But now all awaited his selection of a Queen. After a long pause the Disinherited Knight laid the crown before Rowena. Celdric was "in the height of his joy," and, apart from the disappointed Norman hopefuls, the crowd loudly approved the choice. Even John's craftiness misfired since Fitzurse resented his Prince more than the young knight for the unnecessary insult to his daughter. But the Prince ignored Fitzurse and rode over to invite the new Queen and her champion to that evening's banquet at the Castle of Ashby. Celdric declined for his ward in the Saxon language, which John pretended not to understand and insisted upon having translated into French. The knight also asked to be excused to rest up for the next day's battle. John turned to leave, but his eyes fastened upon the insolent yeoman who had crossed words with him earlier. They repeated their mutual interest in the archery competition, which each hoped would put the other in his place. With that the day ended. Spectators and participants drifted away toward the nearby town of Ashby. The Disinherited Knight went to the pavilion that had been prepared for the prizewinner. And the armorers began their night long chore of repairing the damage of the day's fighting.

Comment

Now that the Disinherited Knight has saved the day, Scott turns our attention to the problem of his identity. He drops two more hints for readers who have not been paying attention. Fitzurse's guess and Isaac's involvement with the knight come very close to giving the mystery away. But the time is not quite ripe to confirm the suspicions of nearly all his readers. Indeed, after the first hint he diverts our attention nicely by introducing a new possibility: Richard may be in England. But once more this is merely the germ of an idea that is not to ripen for several chapters.

Through the Disinherited Knight the Saxons seem to have kept their honor on the field (he may or may not be a Saxon, but he has defeated the Normans). Now they complete their victory in the election of Rowena instead of the prime of Norman maidenhood. Once again (as in Cedric's hall) a Norman attempt to discredit the Saxon race is overthrown and turned into a Saxon triumph. And again the means of victory is an unidentified, apparently disinterested knight.

CHAPTER TEN

Hardly had the Disinherited Knight settled into his new quarters before the squires of the defeated challengers came forward with the horses and armor their masters had forfeited. To four of these he extended "a courtesy and generosity not often practiced," by accepting a mere fifty zecchins apiece to ransom the equipment. From Brian de Bois-Guilbert, however, he would accept nothing: "Say to him in my name that our strife is not ended - no, not till we have fought as well with swords as with lances-as well on foot as on horseback." When the squires had left, the Disinherited Knight instructed his own squire (our old friend Gurth, the swineherd!) to take a bag of gold to Isaac the Jew as payment for the horse and armor he had borrowed. Gurth was unhappy that his master should deal fairly with the untrustworthy Jew, but agreed to meet the old man's price.

Meanwhile in his luxurious apartment at Ashby, the old Jew bemoaned the loss of his purse of gold to the Prince earlier in the day. His daughter reminded him that their race had survived worse calamities and that their wealth was their safekeeping as long as the Gentiles depended upon it. But this only stirred his memory of another probable business loss: the Disinherited Knight's horse and armor had not been paid for. Just then a servant announced a visitor to see Isaac. Gurth was admitted without delay. He explained his master's desire to repay Isaac a just sum for the splendid armor he had worn in the tournament. Much as his emotions had been divided during the jousting, Isaac once more debated "between habitual love of gain and a new-born desire to be liberal" in setting his price. The eighty zecchins he asked was somewhat less than he believed he could get, but only Gurth's shrewdness prevented him from raising the figure as an afterthought. Isaac counted the payment out carefully and overcame an urge to tip the squire or give back a portion of the sum to the young knight. But Gurth was delighted for having saved his master as much again as he had paid for the armor. He had no sooner left Isaac's room than his purse was filled even fuller. Rebecca, who had left the apartment unnoticed by her father, met him as he was leaving and gave him one hundred gold zecchins. Twenty were his, she said, and the rest were to be returned to his master to whom her father owed "deeper kindness than these arms and steed could pay, were their value tenfold." As he made his way up the dark streets of Ashby, Gurth dreamt of two things: the lovely and generous Rebecca (who was beginning to change his opinion of Jews) and the freedom that the tips from his new job might soon buy him.

Comment

One more piece falls into place in the discovery of the Disinherited Knight's identity. He and the Palmer whom we saw last in Chapter VI are one and the same person! The armor he wears is the gift Isaac gave him for saving him from the Templar's cutthroats. But the explanation of Gurth's attachment to this young knight has yet to be given, and his identity therefore officially remains a mystery.

Isaac's apartment is cluttered with the comforts and ornaments which wandering Jews carried with them from their homes in other countries. But even in this familiar environment Isaac continues to be preoccupied with his money. For the third time so far in the novel he is torn between gratitude and greed. And once again Scott makes him the object of derision because of this dilemma. For Gurth and for us, however, Rebecca's restoration of the knight's money removes the bad taste of Isaac's inveterate weakness.

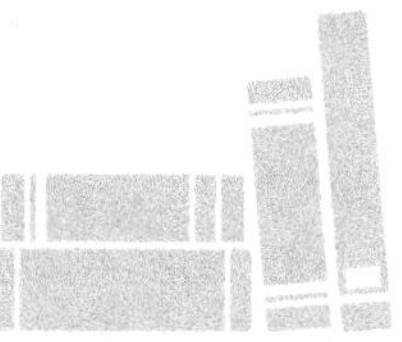

IVANHOE

TEXTUAL ANALYSIS

CHAPTERS 11-16

CHAPTER ELEVEN

The roads out of Ashby were dark and sheltered by low, arching trees. The "distant sound of revelry" in the town alarmed Gurth. Perhaps the Jewess had been right when she cautioned him to "beware how you pass through this crowded town, where thou mayest easily lose both thy burden and thy life." Quickening his step did not help, for he had no sooner reached the thickest part of the bushes than four men surprised him and ordered him to hand over his money. Defiant even in peril, Gurth refused at first. They took him to an opening in the woods where two other thieves awaited them. Here they again demanded his money, which he now admitted amounted to only "thirty zecchins of [his] own property." When he added that the money was to buy his freedom, the robbers said he might as well have spent his money on drink, for it would have made him "as free as thy master, ay, and freer too, if he be a Saxon like thyself." He offered to pay them the whole thirty zecchins in return for his liberty.

But the plan failed when one of the robbers felt the bulging purse beneath his cloak. Now Gurth was forced to admit that his own property was the smaller part of the money he carried. The rest belonged to his master, the Disinherited Knight. This name seemed to please the thieves, who inquired further into the source of the money and the purpose of Gurth's mission. They were astonished at the generosity of the knight in giving his victims such a fair deal; but they refused to believe that a Jewess had returned money to a debtor, until Gurth produced the silk purse Rebecca had given him. As the rest crowded around their captain in disbelief, hoping for a look at the curious proof of Gurth's story, the lusty squire broke loose and pummeled the captain with a quarter-staff in an attempt to escape with his money. His bravery was short-lived, for he was easily subdued once more. But despite the sore head Gurth had given him, the Captain believed his story and regarded him too much like themselves to suffer the loss of his small fortune. Besides, being Saxons themselves, they shared a common enemy in Front-de-Beouf and Bois-Guilbert: "dogs should not worry dogs when wolves and foxes are to be found in abundance." Gurth was not lucky enough to go scot-free, however, for one member of the gang grumbled about "such scruples of conscience" in letting him off so easily. The captain was in a sporting mood and ordered the grumbler-a Miller by trade-to square off with Gurth with quarter staves. Should Gurth win, he was free to pass; lose, and the captain would pay his ransom. "The two champions" armed themselves and peppered one another with insults. Without the pomp but with all the gusto of their betters at the tournament, the swineherd and the miller met in the light of the moon. They fought furiously and nobly, but the swineherd's cool head won the day from his intemperate adversary. After some minutes of combat, Gurth landed a full stroke to the miller's head, "who instantly measured his length upon the green sward." The robbers cheered lustily for the Saxon. They released him and conducted him to the tents outside of the lists, with a warning to tell no one of the night's events. It was a few steps to his knight's tent where Gurth lost no time in relating his astounding adventures. When he had finished, both took their beds in preparation for the work ahead of them.

Comment

This chapter provides a Shakespearean comic relief to the humorless austerity of the main plot. The moonlit joust between Gurth and Miller is an echo of the more exalted duel between the Templar and the Disinherited Knight. Scott emphasizes the mock-heroic quality of the battle scene by apologizing for the "want of a sacred poet to do justice to its eventful progress." His characters utter pompous and bombastic threats (as the knights have done) and his narration takes a higher tone than we have been accustomed to. The humor of such a piece stems from the contrast between the high-flown style and the trivial action it is used to describe. Unfortunately the tone of this chapter is not so much higher than is usual to appear as ridiculous as Scott probably intends it; nor is Gurth's battle as trivial as a mock-heroic demands. Scott's attempts at humor are many, but his successes are few.

CHAPTER TWELVE

The second day of the tournament at Ashby was even more splendid than the first. It was the day of the "general tournament" in which two groups of fifty knights were to fight in the center of the lists simultaneously. Although more dangerous than single jousts, there was no shortage of brave men to volunteer for this mass fighting, all eager to win the day's individual honors for themselves. One of the groups was led by the first day's victor, the Disinherited Knight, and the other by his runner-up, Brian de Bois-Guilbert. About each of these two sides began to gather, depending upon race, politics, personal interest, or confidence in their leader. The Templar's most prominent allies were his fellow challengers of the previous day (Front-de-Boeuf, Malvoisin, et al) and the knights from Prince John's party, including Maurice de Bracy. Oddly enough one Saxon, Athelstane of Coningsburgh, also lined up with the Templar's Norman group. The explanation for his choice had not satisfied Cedric who saw little hope of Saxon glory if her strongest lances were to fight one another. Athelstane's true motive (unknown to Cedric) had nothing to do with Saxon glory. He wanted simply to kill the Disinherited Knight and thus rid himself of a possible rival for Rowena's hand in marriage. Between Cedric and Athelstane the match had long been understood, but no one had troubled to consult the bride about it. Thus no vows had ever passed between him and Rowena-she could favor whom she pleased. Athelstane therefore had good reason to fear the gallantry of this new hero who had named her queen of the tournament; but today he hoped both to eliminate the Disinherited Knight and to win the day's prize for her-a feat that would fortify his claim to the aristocratic Saxon beauty. Opposing these and standing beside the Disinherited Knight were "both English and Norman [knights], natives and strangers."

Rowena, as Queen of Love and Beauty, entered with much fanfare and occupied the throne opposite Prince John's. The marshals again read the rules of combat, after which the two groups of knights ("like so many pillars of iron") filed in, arranging themselves into two rows as they reached the center of the lists. Their armor glittered in the sunlight and colorful streamers fluttered about their weapons and plumed helmets. But as soon as the signal to start the fight was given, the beauty of the pageant vanished. At first the dust stirred by the tumult clouded the field. But when it cleared enough for spectators to make out the fighting, the confusion was staggering. Some men stood, others lay motionless, and some few kept their saddles. The field was strewn with weapons and horses, which obstructed the way of wounded men who sought the safety of the palisades (walls). One side briefly gained an advantage only to lose it quickly. The gallant war-cries and battle sounds "mixed fearfully with the sound of the trumpets, and drowned the groans of those who fell." And in the wreckage and gore of the encounter "what was now visible was only calculated to awaken terror or compassion." No one worried less about the grim change than those who should have noticed it first: the spectators. Well-born ladies cheered their favorites until they were hoarse along with the vulgar mob beneath them. It is all the more understandable, then, that the men felt and acted as though they themselves were taking part in the fighting. Now and then the marshals would shout their encouragement: "Fight on, brave knights! Man dies, but glory lives-death is better than defeat."

On the field, the leaders of the opposing forces had at last singled one another out and begun to answer the previous day's challenge. They had not battled long, however, before Front-de-Boeuf and Athelstane, both doing well on the flanks of their line, decided to join their leader in the destruction of the Disinherited Knight. For all his agility and skillful horsemanship, the knight was hopeless against three such potent warriors. Miraculously, he evaded several attacks but it was clear that he must fall unless Prince John were to intercede for him. But John was deaf to the appeals of the crowd and his own courtiers in behalf of the Disinherited Knight. He had scarcely uttered his refusal to spare him when an incredible turn of events did what John would not. A massive knight in black armor, who had been nicknamed the

Black Sluggard for his listlessness in the early fighting, came to the knight's rescue and with unbelievable strength and efficiency disabled two of his opponents. First he caught Front-de-Boeuf with a sword cut to the head just as "the gigantic arm" was about to strike a blow of its own; then he took Athelstane's own weapon-a battle axe-away from him and clubbed him senseless to the ground with it. The Disinherited's luck took one last turn for the better when Bois-Guilbert's wounded horse finally collapsed under him. But before the helpless Templar could be forced to yield, Prince John stopped the contest and "the Gentle and Joyous Passage of Arms of Ashby" faded into history.

As in the search for a queen the day before, John's choice for the day's honors conflicted with the general will. He ordered that the prize be bestowed upon the Black Sluggard, since the Disinherited Knight could not have prevailed without him. This time he would have won his point, but the Sluggard disappeared as abruptly as he had come. Now there could be no question about the winner. For the second day in a row the Disinherited Knight advanced to receive the reward for his prowess. This time he knelt before the Queen of his choice to receive the Chaplet of Honour from her own hands. She commanded that his helmet be removed to receive the crown properly. The marshals ignored the knight's weak protests and carried out her order. At the sight of the fair-haired, sunburnt youth, Rowena stifled a shriek. And as she set the crown upon his head, it was the worthy Ivanhoe who fainted from the wounds of battle before her.

Comment

The open secret that Scott has withheld from his readers for many chapters after most of them had guessed it is a last revealed. The Disinherited Knight, alias the Palmer, is none other than the banished son of Cedric, the lover of Rowena, the youngest of Richard's heroic knights, Wilfred of Ivanhoe. But Scott prefers that his readers have such a puzzle to engage them, so before he solves the young knight's identity he poses that of the mysterious Black Knight. The incredible power and size of this figure and the feat of brushing aside two of the strongest warriors in England mark him for prominence in the novel. The unevenness of his temperament and fighting spirit is also peculiar. One minute he behaves like a disinterested spectator, and another he is unquestionably the most ferocious fighter on the field. As before, however, direct confrontation of his identity is deferred until a more strategic moment.

For the third time Ivanhoe and Bois-Guilbert fail to finish their duel fairly (the other times were at Ashby, and Acre in the Holy Land). Although Ivanhoe has beaten him twice, both contests were decided more by the failure of the Templar's equipment than by the superiority of either man. A similar situation occurs in *Quentin Durward*, Chapter 37, where again the hero closes in battle with his greatest foe after a desperate search for him in the chaos of battle, but never does succeed in killing him. Welsh (see bibliography) observes that Scott never allows his heroes to soil their hands with the blood of their enemies.

Prior to Stendhal and Tolstoy, novelists rarely attempted to depict mass battle scenes. When it became necessary or desirable to describe a battle, it was usually accomplished in the manner of the **epic** poets, who saw war as a series of glorious duels between individual heroes rather than as general, indiscriminate slaughter (See *Iliad, Aeneid,* Shakespeare's histories, and compare to *Charterhouse of Parma* and *War and Peace*). Scott's treatment of war is neither classical nor modern, but characteristically his own. He focuses upon one important duel, in the manner of the **epic** writers. But he says enough about the general clash to betray an ironical condemnation of war. First he makes the shocking contrast between the beauty and symmetry of the warriors' procession and the ugly mess that follows it. Then, after numbering the dead, the dying, and the maimed, says that "Hence it is always mentioned in the old records as the Gentle and Joyous Passage of Arms at Ashby." The **irony** is heavy-handed, but the author's sentiments are unmistakable.

Scott stages this melee, then, not for love of war but for two other reasons: 1) he wishes to raise the combat from a purely personal to an ideological level, in order to 2) redefine the issues that divided Englishmen. The first day was primarily an occasion for the Disinherited Knight's glorification. Since he carried the hopes of the oppressed Saxon race with him, as well, the net effect of his success was a Norman defeat. On this day, however, the traditional division between Norman and Saxon does not hold up when the warriors choose sides.

Athelstane, a Saxon, joins the Norman confederates of Prince John, while brave men of both races support the Disinherited Knight. What Scott seems to be doing is realigning Englishmen according to moral and nationalistic standards. The true division between Englishmen, he implies, is not Norman vs. Saxon, but good vs. evil, toleration vs. bigotry, patriotism vs. self-interest. A man's genuine allegiance belongs to his nation, not to his race. Athelstane is the key to this change, for he disregards the honor of his people in favor of his private and one-sided feud with the Disinherited Knight, just as Normans with whom he sides have betrayed Richard to pursue their own private ends: wealth, beauty, and power.

Scott is hard at work in this chapter developing two characters who never amount to much as the novel proceeds: Prince John and Athelstane. For the second time he shows us the tactlessness of Prince John, who is so devoid of political intelligence that he may be considered the antithesis of Louis XI in *Quentin Durward*. John is just as devious and cunning as the French king, but nowhere near so successful. Only perversity could have persuaded him to withhold the prize from the Disinherited Knight, although his selection of the Black Sluggard is intensely ironic in view of later developments. Athelstane has displayed dullness, stupidity, and spite on the two occasions we have met him-a character entirely uncomplicated by noble virtues. Scott discredits him solely for the purpose of changing Cedric's stubborn mind about two things: 1) his suitability as a husband for Rowena; and 2) his importance as a symbol of past Saxon glory. It is largely by the character of Athelstane that Scott avoids a naively melodramatic conflict between good Saxons and bad Normans in his novel.

CHAPTER THIRTEEN

When the name of Ivanhoe reached him, Prince John congratulated himself on the intuition that had caused him uneasiness in the young knight's presence the day before. The others around him thought of a more immediate danger: what would become of the manor King Richard had given to Ivanhoe, but which it had pleased John to reassign to Front-de-Boeuf in the knight's absence? Front-de Boeuf was powerful and would not relinquish it easily. First John reminded them of his "right" to reward those loyal to, and available to serve, their country, even if it meant depriving "those who have wandered to foreign countries". Since most of his company had either benefited by this axiom or soon hoped to, his words were greeted with a cheer. Even Prior Aymer agreed, inasmuch as the Crusaders could not be considered to be doing Christians' work since they fell short of capturing the Holy City. When reports of the grave condition of the wounded Ivanhoe arrived, the issue seemed well closed. The Prince would have made more certain of this by ordering his own physician to his bedside, but Fitzurse said Ivanhoe "was already removed from the lists, and in the custody of his friends."

The mood of the Prince's party brightened somewhat as they talked of Rowena, who had been so brave in stifling her emotions when her lover fell before her. Aymer added an account of her wealth to his praise of her beauty, which the Prince thought made her an excellent match for a Norman. De Bracy was the lucky man he chose to be her husband. And to seal the bargain he arranged to invite "Rowena and her company" to a banquet at the Castle of Ashby that night.

As he gave this order the Prince received a note, decorated with the emblem of Philip of France, warning him that Richard was free. Despite the panic that gripped him, John (who "looked like a man who has received news that a sentence of execution has been passed upon him") listened to Fitzurse's advice. There would have to be a meeting of their forces at York to head off the threat of Richard's imminent return. For now, the commoners' contests would have to be cut short and the tournament ended. As a consolation to the "herd of Saxon serfs," and a sweet revenge for the Prince, only the archery competition would take place. John spotted the "insolent peasant" whom he had challenged to shoot against his best bowmen, and dared him to enter. The wager he offered was hardly attractive. If the yeoman won, the Prince would add a cash prize to the silver bugle offered; if he lost, he would be disgraced, beaten, and driven from the lists. Despite the terms, the yeoman (whose name was Locksley) accepted the challenge.

Hubert, the best of the king's archers, defeated the other entries by a wide margin. Against Locksley he aimed long and sure and sent two shafts into the heart of the target. The first was a bit off center, however, and Locksley (who shot "as if he had not even looked at the mark") laid one two inches closer to dead center. Hubert's second shot "alighted in the very center of the target," but again the yeoman improved upon this seemingly perfect shot: he splintered Hubert's arrow. Not satisfied with this target, Locksley set up a rod the thickness of a man's thumb at a distance of one hundred yards from his mark. Hubert refused even to attempt the shot. But Locksley-good-naturedly repeating Hubert's favorite expression, "A man can do but his best" - took careful aim this time and split the rod. Even Prince John gasped in admiration of his skill: "never did so strong a hand bend a bow, or so true an eye direct a shaft." Forgetting their earlier exchange, he offered Locksley a post among his private guard. But the Yeoman had vowed to serve only King Richard. He accepted the bugle, but gave the cash prize to Hubert, "who would have hit the wand as well as I" but for modesty. Then he disappeared into the crowd, unnoticed by John. For at that moment the prince was dispatching an urgent message to Isaac the Jew, demanding a loan of 2,000 crowns payable at York within six days.

Comment

Now that Ivanhoe's identity is known, Scott does not permit us to linger over him. There is no reunion with Rowena, no reconciliation with his father. Indeed, we have only the cunning Fitzurse's word that Ivanhoe is with friends. Instead Scott raises new problems and resolves an old one. The focus shifts to John's party. Rowena has thus far survived the hot stare of Bois-Guilbert and Athelstane's clumsy attempt to win her, but now we meet another of Ivanhoe's rivals for her favor: Prince John promises her to De Bracy. This is the most important event in the chapter from the standpoint of the plot. The promise causes De Bracy to desire Rowena and, eventually, to abduct her when John cannot get her for him. But two other important lines of development are also at work.

The archery contest is one of the most famous sporting events in literature. Scott himself draws the parallel to the funeral games for Patroclos in the *Iliad*. Perhaps an even closer Homeric relative is the bow of Odysseus, which only he can draw, and with which he rides his house of suitors after his return. Within twenty years after Scott's scene appeared in print, James Fenimore Cooper adapted it to the American frontier for one of his most memorable scenes: the shooting match in The Pathfinder. If Locksley's marksmanship seems difficult to believe, Scott's authority in the *Robin Hood* **Ballads** goes even further:

Robin Hood was an archer good, And he drew a lusty strong bow, He could shoot two north country miles and an inch, As the Pinder of Wakefield doth know.

In the context of the novel, it is one more of a series of defeats and humiliations the Normans suffer at Ashby - this one at the level of the commoner. This scene also contains the most conspicuous of many anachronisms (historical inaccuracies) in the novel. The longbow did not achieve this kind of efficiency as a weapon until the century after the action of this book. But whatever Locksley's feat may lack of history, as sheer adventure it needs no apology.

The event that dominates this chapter, however, is not Ivanhoe's wound, De Bracy's betrothal, or even the archery contest. It is rather the startling news of Richard's release from captivity. Scott sets the scene for this news by catching Prince John at his most arrogant and disrespectful of the King's law. The case in point is Ivanhoe's estate-a gift from Richard-, now the property of Front-de-Boeuf by the grace of John's will. Shortly after defending his confiscation of the lands of Richard's crusading supporters (the castle of Ashby is another example), John is toppled from his arrogance by the message from Philip. He may boast: "Were this my last hour of power, it should be a hour sacred to revenge and pleasure." But his expression and frantic message to Isaac tell another story.

CHAPTER FOURTEEN

Prince John's banquet at the castle of Ashby was a splendid affair. He hoped to impress his guests, Norman and Saxon, with the luxury of his table, and to flatter them with the gentility of his manner. For it was clear that he needed all the support he could get now that Richard was on his way home. But John was not a man to persist in this kind of politicking without revealing his true feelings, and losing all his deception had won. He had proved this years ago in Ireland when, as an ambassador of his father, King Henry II, his insults to the natives wrecked any hope of English domination there. Now his own fortune depended upon the evenness of his temper.

Cedric and Athelstane arrived with apologies for Rowena's absence. They wore "the ancient Saxon garb," which was in fact far more practical though less fashionable than the Norman dress. But soon their clothing and the indelicacy of their table manners were the butt of whispered jests and ridicule around the table. After a sumptuous meal John proposed a toast to Ivanhoe. Cedric declined to drink because of the disobedience of the knight he once called "son" in leaving home to join Richard's court and later his Crusade. Thinking he had found an ideal solution to the settlement of Ivanhoe's estate, John asked whether Cedric would not rather see Richard's reward to his son confiscated and given to Front-de-Boeuf. But before the Saxon could answer, Front-de-Boeuf defied any man to take what was his as if he were a mere Saxon. Cedric was stung by the slur and retaliated. By now John's assumed politeness had worn thin and he chimed in with an insult to the Saxon's outlandish clothes. Soon every Norman around the table had added an insult to Cedric, as the old man seethed before them. Fitzurse alone realized the insanity of this course and arranged a brief truce between Norman and Saxon. In a show of bogus good will John invited Cedric to drink to a Norman as he had drunk to a Saxon. Fitzurse was quickly at Cedric's back, advising him to name John in the toast to erase any hard feelings between them. But instead Cedric dedicated his toast to "the best and noblest of his race," Richard the Lion-hearted! His words jarred the Norman throng and divided them between loyalty to their lawful king and to the usurper, John. Some, imitating their Prince, returned their goblets to the table. Many others drank heartily and cheered the king. But none dared to object to the tribute the Saxon had accorded their sovereign. "Having enjoyed his triumph for a minute," Cedric collected Athelstane and left the conspirators to fight among themselves. John was angry and dumbfounded at the extent of the Saxon victory: "[the] churls have borne off the best of the day, and have retreated with triumph." Even as he was speaking, the guests began to leave the hall; only a few of his closest advisers stayed behind to comfort him in despair. Fitzurse assured his Prince that he and De Bracy could rally "these shuffling cowards," but John thought only of his certain defeat now that his partisans had left him. "Unhappy are the counselors of a Prince," Fitzurse pined, "who wants fortitude and perseverance alike in good and evil."

Comment

This chapter and the next give us a rare insight into the character of the Prince and his conspiracy. Scott puts into words what has already become apparent in John's actions: even his cleverest plots are ruined by the "levity and petulance" of his temper. Before the chapter is over we learn that he is also infirm of purpose-hardly a man fit to rule England.

Scott plainly dislikes the snobbery that "fashions" promote. He stresses the utility of "unfashionable" Saxon dress and the common sense of their "unrefined" manners (they wipe their greasy hands on a towel instead of waving them in the air to dry). Correspondingly, the Normans' tastes seem vain and impractical. Even their cuisine typifies the excess of artifice in Norman life by "rendering [foods] perfectly unlike their natural appearance." And although he is an exception, the forecast of John's death from overeating speaks rather badly for Norman manners.

CHAPTER FIFTEEN

The real genius behind the Norman conspiracy was Fitzurse. Like a spider repairing his web he busily drew back into line the irresolute members of John's "cabal" (group of fellow-plotters) who had been shaken by Cedric's toast. For each man he had a different argument, and above all the threat that Richard's return would go hard with them whether they gave up now or not. He even had an argument for John's title to the throne. Since Richard's right to reign was not clear, they had the right to choose the man who suited them best. And clearly John's generosity was preferable to Richard's vengeance. By the end of his night's work Fitzurse had persuaded most of the faction to convene at York "for the purpose of making general arrangements for placing the crown upon the head of Prince John."

When Fitzurse met with De Bracy back at the castle he was astonished to find him dressed in the outfit of an English yeoman, complete with cap, sword, and longbow and arrows. Why had he not been out doing the Prince's work? What purpose for the masquerade? De Bracy threw Fitzurse's scolding back at him: "Come, Fitzurse, we know each other-ambition is thy pursuit, pleasure mine, and they become our different ages." They both served John only as long as it sped their private interests. Tonight De Bracy planned to take his interest into his own hands by abducting Rowena in the manner that Prior Aymer's tale the night before had recommended for men deprived of their brides. Fitzurse attempted to discourage this undertaking for its poor timing and the bad feeling it would create among the Saxons. And when he learned that the Templar, Bois-Guilbert, had helped to hatch the plan, he warned De Bracy that he had more to fear from his friend than from his enemies. But the impassioned knight had no patience for advice. He would be disguised and his plan was sound. "Farewell," he said, "I go, like a true knight, to win the smiles of beauty." As Fitzurse watched him go he reflected on the unreliability of his associates ("tools"). Even John, the beneficiary of his efforts, could not be depended on to serve his own best interests. But even a Prince would learn to yield to Fitzurse in time. These words had barely left his mouth when a call from John sent him scurrying "to receive the orders of the future sovereign."

Comment

This chapter belongs to Fitzurse, a character in the tradition of Odysseus, Machiavelli, and Scott's own Louis XI. He is the type of the crafty, unscrupulous politician, who places the interests of his state before any consideration of moral right and wrong. He is a man who manipulates others in any way he can. His only standard is the success of his sovereign's policies.

The brilliance of John's counselor nearly obscures the next important link in the plot. Cedric's angry departure from Ashby has obviously cost De Bracy a fine wife. Now Cedric would never consent to a match between his ward and a Norman. While Fitzurse is out rounding up John's timid allies, therefore, De Bracy disguises himself for the purpose of snatching Rowena. The involvement of Bois-Guilbert in the plot raises the possibility that he is also after Rowena. De Bracy may only be a dupe in the Templar's designs upon her. But for now these shadows seem far off, and De Bracy is too full of gusto and chivalric daydreams to anticipate them.

Indeed, one of the most striking distinctions between De Bracy and John's other principal lieutenants is his relative lack of sinister motive and vicious character. He is a kidnapper, but like his Homeric prototype, Paris, he regards his actions as exceptionally gallant. He never doubts that Rowena will love him of her own free will; the abduction merely makes that love possible by avoiding Cedric's censorship. This is partially illustrated by the fact that Aymer's fractured tale has given De Bracy the courage and the sanction to commit this grave act. For all his military bearing, De Bracy is an adolescent in matters of love, taking his cue from romantic stories rather than from the hard realities that preoccupy men like Fitzurse.

CHAPTER SIXTEEN

Meanwhile the Black Knight, who had vanished from the lists before he could receive the prize, found it heavy going on his journey away from Ashby. The first night he spent "at a small hostelry," but as the following evening closed on him after a hard day's ride he had found no lodgings to rest in. Indeed he was all but lost in the thickness of the woods. Most knights would have taken this opportunity to sprawl beneath a tree and dream of their lady fair. This one chose instead to give his horse his head to lead them wherever his instinct might detect supper and a bed. The horse justified his master's trust, for they soon came within earshot of a tinkling chapel bell, and shortly to the tiny, ruined chapel itself and a rude hut nearby. The Black Knight's knock at the door of the hut produced a voice that told him to pass on. Only when he threatened to burst the door's hinges could the hermit within be persuaded to unlock. He turned out to be "a large, strong-built man," a monk who called himself the Clerk of Copmanhurst. For supper he offered the knight parched peas and water; but from the size of the Friar's mouth and teeth this seemed "miserable grist for so large and able a mill." The knight could not help but wonder how his host maintained his strapping body on such poor fare: "You appear a man more fit to win the ram at a wrestling match." As their strangeness eased, the Friar had a sudden recollection that a forest keeper had left him some other food. Before long they had not only consumed a large pasty (meat pie) of venison, but washed it down with several hearty cups of wine. The Black Knight was perplexed at this wonder and the mystery of so worldly a body buried deep in the forest. He probed into the Friar's secrets until warned to stop, and then he probed further. The angry Friar gave him his choice of weapons, since he would not be content with less. And when he opened a second cupboard (the first held the food) the Knight stared in amazement at the Friar's arsenal. This display was answer enough to all his questions, and instead of swords the Knight picked a harp that lay among the weapons and offered instead to prove his skill with it. Satisfied at this reply, the Friar filled their cups in good fellowship once more and prepared to "drink, sing and be merry."

Comment

This is one of the most delightful confrontations in Srott's novels. Its interest lies in the gradual disclosure of the Friar's true means and, eventually, his identity. But for now it is sufficient to watch the growth of respect and understanding between two such extraordinary men. The Friar's ludicrous attempts to send the stranger away, and then to conceal the riches of his cupboard, make him appear a fool at first. His change of heart is embarrassingly obvious and we must laugh at his dilemma when he produces food that his religious vows prevent him from eating. Granting the obvious differences, his appeal here is similar to Falstaff's (the comic character from Shakespeare's *Henry IV*, Part 1, etc.): a thoroughgoing but lovable scoundrel, caught in a barefaced lie. But when the Black Knight pushes too far, we gain a surprising awareness of the Friar's decidedly un-Falstaffian skill at arms and readiness to employ it against those who take him lightly. We must approve of the Knight's discretion in offering to play a song rather than oppose such a formidable enemy. (Far from implying softness or cowardice, the knight's singing ability is consistent with the best heroic and chivalric traditions in the classics. Achilles, the hero of Homer's *Iliad*, is only the first of a long history of singing heroes that persists to this day in the crooning cowboys of the films.)

The mystery of the Black Knight, deferred for several chapters, resumes in this one. Except for a look at his face we are nowhere nearer to his identity than before. Like Cedric, he is a blond; but his moustaches are black: he is neither a Saxon nor a Norman, by the rule of thumb we've noticed about the coloring of Scott's characters.

Consideration for his horse is only one of the chivalric virtues he demonstrates to us and the Friar. More noteworthy, perhaps, is his un-knightly contempt for the romantic **conventions** of courtly and chivalric love. This is not a man to waste his valuable time dreaming of a distant mistress when doubt and adversity bar his way. The Black Knight puts his trust in nature and fortune-but he is too alert and realistic to wait for the night to swallow him.

In this first chapter after Ashby, Scott begins the lengthy task of drawing his principal characters-dispersed after the tournament-toward the next convergence, or **climax**. We shall examine this in detail later, but for now it is sufficient to observe that even in this self-contained **episode** Scott is advancing the larger structural design of his novel.

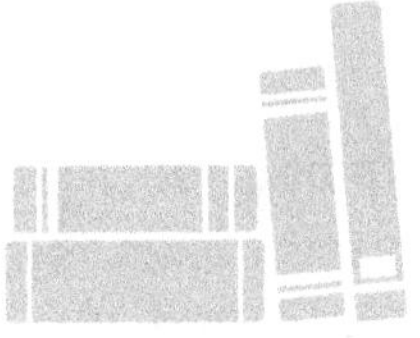

IVANHOE

TEXTUAL ANALYSIS

CHAPTERS 17-22

CHAPTER SEVENTEEN

After the harp had been tuned (with some difficulty), the knight struck up a "**ballad** composed by a Saxon glee-man (minstrel), whom I knew in Holy Land." What his voice lacked of natural quality, training had more than supplied. His song, "The Crusader's Return," told of a knight returned from the fighting, shorn of everything but his armor and his honor, asking that his lady fair admit him to her castle since his gallantry in her name has brought her widespread fame. The Friar sat like an opera critic throughout the performance, and applauded when it was through. He disapproved of a Saxon minstrel's adopting such a melancholy Norman style, but he drank "to the success of all true lovers." The Friar's song, "The Barefooted Friar," was boisterous and bawdy. It celebrated the unholy privileges and diversions of his own calling, especially the various kinds of charity a monk could expect from his congregation (or, rather, those believers whose homes he visited). Not a knight - nor even a king, ever had it so good, he says. When the stranger questioned the piety behind so lusty a song, the Friar listed the religious duties he performed to ward off the forces of evil. But the subject was a touchy one and the Friar quickly dismissed it from their conversation. Their songs and mirth multiplied until "their revels were interrupted by a loud knocking at the door."

Comment

Scott develops the contrast between these two men by having each sing a characteristic song. Although we learned in the last chapter that the knight is more warrior than lover, his songs is typical of the **conventions** of courtly love. Scott is probably ironic once again in coupling the lofty sentiments of the lover in the song with the barbaric deeds he has done in love's name. There is certainly more of wisdom in the Friar's common sense reaction to the song: "What took the honest knight from home? Or what could he expect but to find his mistress engaged of a rival on his return. . . ." And even his conciliatory toast "to the success of all true lovers" is no concession to the sentiments of the song, for it was a cardinal rule of courtly love that the lover must never "succeed" with his lady. Although Scott eventually arranges for the union to two lovers, we never see their bliss; his interest, consistent with the courtly love tradition, is more in the pain of unfulfilled love than in the pleasure of "success." The Friar's song is, in effect, an answer to the knight's. It ridicules the absurd ideals of chivalry and places religion before monarchy as a means to the happy life. The Friar is without a care, for he can depend upon his cloth to fetch him a woman or a hot meal whenever the appetite seizes him. Scott never came closer to the spirit of Boccaccio, the great Italian storyteller, whose tales of earthly love and sensual delights often involved priests and nuns in principal roles. However different their station in the church, the Saxon Friar and the Norman Prior Aymer (Chapter II) are equally scandalous in the abuse of their holy office, although hardly exceptional among their colleagues. The important difference between them is in the degree and object of their violations. Aymer is a powerful and wealthy man whose corruption and hypocrisy may work to stamp out a noble race (remember that he is a close adviser to John and an intimate of the Templar). Our Friar is, after all, a hermit, so we never see him behave badly. His instincts are more appealing than the Prior's because they are open, natural, free of the vanities Aymer is so fond of. And it is easier to believe that the Friar sees no contradiction between his habits and his vows. Aymer may see none either, but he should. One last distinction between the two singers: the knight sings with a cultivated voice and, by the choice of songs he offers the Friar, he reveals a considerable formal knowledge of the art; the Friar sings without art and prefers the freer "derry-down chorus." (Note: the source of the knight's song is the first indication we have had that he, like Ivanhoe and the Templar, is a returning Crusader.)

Scott's reference to Ariosto at the end of the chapter is important for several reasons. It reveals his fondness for this great Italian poet (whose Orlando Furioso is the greatest of Romance **epics** and a textbook of chivalric lore). It also tells us something about the particular use he has made of Ariosto's work-here, in a matter of plot construction. More important, it is Scott's way of excusing his poorly woven plot. The fact that he has three or four main plot lines working simultaneously makes it impossible for him to keep abreast of all his characters without switching abruptly from plot to plot. At Ashby he drew our attention to Prince John's headaches; now he has picked up the Black Knight in his wandering through a forest; next he will bring us up to date on Cedric, and later on Isaac, and finally on Ivanhoe himself. But with so many divergent stories to follow, even Ariosto would have been hard put to reunite them.

CHAPTER EIGHTEEN

Even when Ivanhoe collapsed at Rowena's feet, Cedric refused to recognize him as his son. But he did arrange to help the young man get back to Ashby. The servants he sent to aid Ivanhoe, however, soon reported back that his body was gone. According to bystanders, he "had been raised with care by certain well-attired grooms and placed in a litter belonging to a lady among the spectators." Hearing that his son was in good hands, Cedric's "paternal anxiety . . . gave way anew to the feeling of injured pride and resentment. . . ." The servants did succeed, however, in recapturing Gurth, whom Cedric regarded as a deserter. The faithful swineherd-turned-squire has also been searching for his wounded master, but without regard for his own safety.

Rowena was so angry at Cedric's refusal to be reconciled to Ivanhoe that she refused to attend Prince John's banquet. And when, after storming out of the banquet hall later that evening, Cedric first saw Gurth, he heaped his anger upon the helpless serf. He abused him and had him bound like a common criminal without hearing any explanation. Then Cedric ordered his party to the Convent at St. Withold's where they spent a comfortable evening. As they prepared to leave for Rotherwood (Cedric's hall) the next morning, however, a large black dog howling at the convent gate frightened the superstitious Saxons. Impatient to be off, Cedric cast his spear at this unlucky omen. He had recognized the dog as Fangs, Gurth's "faithful adherent," and narrowly missed killing him. No torture, no injury could have embittered Gurth against Cedric more than this naked act of cruelty to a dumb animal. He renounced his master on the spot.

Back on the trail, Cedric and Athelstane talked about the recent improvement in prospects for Saxon liberation, now that dissension among the Norman leaders had come to the surface.

One problem they faced was the choice of a chief to unite and spearhead the resurgence. Both Athelstane and Rowena were of royal blood, but the other Saxon leaders disagreed as to which of the two had the better title to the throne. Cedric had unselfishly withdrawn his own name from consideration (despite his obvious qualifications for the job and popularity among his people) and attempted to eliminate the doubts of his countrymen by "promoting a marriage betwixt Rowena and Athelstane." Hence "the original cause of the banishment of Wilfred" was that his romance with Rowena obstructed the interests of the Saxon race, in Cedric's opinion. Ivanhoe had been relatively easy to eliminate; but to this day Cedric found it impossible to bend Rowena's will to favor a match with Athelstane. She was not ambitious for a throne and she detested Athelstane; moreover she had the advantage of royal blood to protect her freedom of choice: Ivanhoe's return and victory in the lists had warmed and gratified Cedric as a father, but it was "almost a death's blow to his hopes" as a patriot. Rowena would be harder to convince than ever now that her favorite had returned in glory. The unexpected change of fortune at the banquet, however, inspired him to make one last effort to arrange the marriage. But as they talked, he found Athelstane as "Unready" as ever: willing to accept the throne, but too lazy to work for it. And when he dropped back to confer with Rowena, her impudent maid insisted upon recalling Athelstane's defeat in the lists-a fact that made Cedric's difficult mission all but impossible. In all, the day had been full of "displeasure and discomfort" for the Saxon statesman.

Comment

For the second time Scott alludes to Saxon superstitions. Gurth nearly took Rebecca for a ghost in Chapter X, and here Fangs is mistaken for an evil omen. Or is it a mistake? Irrational and crude as these fears may be, simple men often have an instinct for future danger. The superficial resemblance between Cedric's wounding of Fangs and the murder of the albatross in Coleridge's Rime of the Ancient Mariner ends at the question of belief. Scott had no faith in dark, supernatural forces that shape men's lives, but he knew what made for a good story. When Fangs turns out to have been, in fact, an omen of evil (when the train is attacked), it is not a proof of the superstition but the hand of Providence upon a man who has sinned.

This chapter contains the most extensive and authoritative treatment of Wilfred's banishment from his father's house. Earlier we heard rumors that Cedric was jealous of his son's love for the beautiful Rowena; then Cedric himself claimed the boy had been disobedient in joining Richard's court and following him to the Holy Land. But there is no doubt that the fundamental reason for Cedric's action was the political one described here.

CHAPTER NINETEEN

The travelers entered the forest late in the day unafraid of the outlaws who might lurk there. Aside from their numbers (twelve fighting men), they relied for their protection upon the supposition that outlaws were usually impoverished Saxons who would do their countrymen no harm. Before long they came upon another smaller party that had been abandoned in the forest by its body-guard. Athelstane instantly recognized the Jew, Isaac, who had insulted them at Ashby. His daughter, Rebecca, the only other person in sight, sat beside the horse-litter "of a sick friend." Their hired servants, Isaac explained, had run off with the horses and mules when they heard that outlaws were lying in wait for the old Jew. But his appeal for help was wasted on Athelstane, who considered the plunder and outrage they faced a proper reward for "bearding" (defying) their betters at the tournament. Cedric could not agree with his companion, however, and proposed to leave men and horses enough to get the wretched Jews to safety. This would have been their final course had Rebecca not come forward. She kissed the hem of Rowena's gown and begged her to allow them to join their party for the sake of the sick man in the litter, "dear even to you." Rowena yielded as much to the girl's nobility as to the strength of her appeal. With Cedric's consent, the Jews and the litter were mounted and allowed to ride in the rear of the column. But while the train was adding to its numbers, it lost an old face. Gurth, with some assistance from Wamba (he loosened the ropes), scampered into the bushes unnoticed and disappeared from sight.

Somewhat later, as the travelers reached a narrow passage, they were attacked on all sides by a band of outlaws. Only Wamba, the poor jester, was able to give a good account of himself against them, and he alone escaped into the woods. Within moments Gurth and Fangs, who had been following the action, joined forces with him. Now that his master's fortune had changed, Gurth was eager to serve him once more. Two serfs and a crippled dog, they prepared to rescue their friends from the armed band. Just as they were about to "attack," a third figure intercepted them and demanded to know what had happened. He was dressed, like the outlaws, in a forest-green blouse, but the bugle horn he carried identified him to Wamba as Locksley, the champion bowman at Ashby. On his command, they waited while he mingled with the robbers, learned their plans, and returned to recommend a counter-plan. By now Gurth had begun to recognize the man's voice as that of the outlaw captain who had used him so fairly on the first night of the tournament. And when this stranger proposed they postpone their foolhardy rescue until he could gather a stronger force to aid them, the good impression Gurth had formed of him induced him to agree. Wamba had no such comfort, however, and followed with great reluctance.

Comment

This important chapter brings together a number of the novel's sub-plots and, by means of the attack, divides them again into two clearcut groups. First Rebecca and Isaac (along with their litter) join Cedric; then his entire party is engulfed by De Bracy's cutthroats, disguised as yeomen. Wamba and Gurth escape and meet Locksley, who also turns out to be the outlaw chief from Ashby. With these two groups about which to build a war, the siege of Torquilstone (the next important pillar of the action) is effectively under way even before we see the castle.

It is one of the minor ironies of the book that Gurth and Wamba, a pair of serfs, finds themselves free men, while the mighty Cedric and Athelstane are humbled by their captivity.

CHAPTER TWENTY

Locksley conducted Cedric's serfs to a great oak where six of his men had been waiting for him. He asked after the other members of his band. The Miller, he was told, was on his way to Rotherham "with six men and good hope of booty." Alan-a-Dale was out watching for the Prior of Jourvaulx (Aymer), and the Friar was still in his cell. Hearing this, the Captain (as Locksley is called at this point) decided to alert the Friar next. Briefly he instructed his men in their several duties. They were to meet him at daybreak with as many men as they could find. Two men were sent towards Front-de Boeuf's castle at Torquilstone to watch "a set of gallants, who have been masquerading in such guise as our own, [and] are carrying prisoners thither." When Locksley and his companions reached the Friar's, they were surprised to hear a jolly drinking song coming from the hut. It was several moments before Locksley's knocks penetrated to the drunken. Friar and his equally drunken guest, the Black Knight, Assuming their visitors to be strange travelers they hurriedly removed the evidence of their feast and wassail (drinking party) and changed their tune to a solemn religious hymn. But the Friar eventually recognized the voice outside the door and admitted Locksley and his friends. At first the knight and the outlaw captain regarded one another with suspicion. Before long Locksley recognized him as the savior of the Disinherited Knight at Ashby and, somewhat reassured, asked whether he was "as well a good Englishman as a good Knight." The knight's reply could not have been more satisfactory and to the point: "You can speak to no one to whom England, and the life of every Englishman, can be dearer than to me." Now that they understood each other, Locksley imparted the news of Cedric's capture and their plans to rescue him the next morning. Would he join their assault? "I am bound by my vow to do so," he answered. Although both men preferred to conceal their names, they sealed the agreement with mutual trust. Even Wamba was heartened by the addition of so noble an ally. The knight and the Friar, who had by now removed his vestments and replaced them with the forest green of Locksley's yeomen, shook off "all marks of the midnight revel" by washing in a frosty fountain near the hut. As they prepared to march, the Black Knight was startled at the name of their destination: "What! is it Front-de-Boeuf who has stopt in the king's highway the king's liege subjects?' 'Opressor he ever was,' said Locksley." Locksley's respect for "decency and prudence" prevented the Friar from saying more of Front-de Boeuf's crimes. On this grim note they struck out for the rendezvous with the remainder of Locksley's band.

Comment

With this chapter, all the principal rescuers have joined in the adventure. Gurth and Wamba, the Black Knight, and Locksley's band will form the attack force. Except for Wamba, whose pessimism is slow to yield, each man respects and supports his comrades-all are prepared for a unified assault upon Torquilstone. The latest addition, the Black Knight, still refuses to be named, although his heartfelt answer to Locksley's test of his patriotism, and his familiarity with Front-de-Boeuf, are hazy forecasts of his identity.

For the second time in the novel Scott helps his reader to keep track of the action by means of a concrete reference point. In Chapters II & III it was the Templar's bugle sound; here it is Locksley's knock on the Friar's door. The knock first occurred in Chapter XVII. It has taken Scott three chapters to bring Cedric and his company up to this same point in time, and he reminds us of it be repeating the same knock. Any complex novel poses problems of this sort for its author. But Scott could hardly have chosen a clumsier solution than the one he uses here. His general plan is to organize the action of the book around several crucial incidents or scenes. As each of these scenes occurs it is necessary to explain the career of every character who will figure importantly in it. Preparatory to the siege of Torquilstone, the central **episode** of the novel, no fewer than five major flashbacks interrupt the action, not to mention a number of bothersome but less obstructive "background" passages. Scott has never been thought of as a master of plot construction (as, for example, Fielding and Jane Austen, among English novelists, are) but Ivanhoe must be among his less successful creations in this respect.

CHAPTER TWENTY-ONE

As Cedric's rescuers were gathering, the prisoners were hurried toward Torquilstone castle under the goading of their guards. The leaders of this expedition, De Bracy and the Templar (Bois-Guilbert), discussed the next step in their plot. The original plan called for De Bracy to "rescue" Rowena from Torquilstone. Since she had seen him only in disguise among the bandits, her gratitude to De Bracy would be limitless-certainly to the point of marrying her courageous deliverer. But De Bracy had thought better of this plan since Fitzurse warned him of the Templar's treachery. Instead of parting company with the outlaws, therefore, he decided to continue to the castle, insuring that the Templar would keep his word. Once there, he would make a clean breast of his passion to Rowena, who he hoped would pardon "the violence of which I have been guilty." The Templar indignantly denied De Bracy's suspicions, claiming to be far more interested in the beautiful Rebecca than in Rowena. But De Bracy was only partially satisfied, and insisted upon his change in plans. Cedric meanwhile tried to reason with his "Saxon" captors for having abused a friend to their cause. He realized the futility of his plea as soon as the "hoary and ancient castle of Reginald Front-de-Boeuf," Torquilstone, appeared beyond the trees. These were Norman mercenaries (hired soldiers) disguised as honest Saxon yeomen. He saw the cleverness of their plan: to conceal their own responsibility for the crime while discrediting the English yeomanry.

Inside the castle the prisoners were sorted into groups and sent to quarters that best suited the purposes of their jailers. The great hall of the castle - now a guardroom - received the Saxon chiefs, Athelstane and Cedric. The castle had once belonged to Torquil Wolfganger, a great Saxon lord before the Conquest, who had given it his name. For Cedric it was full of memories of that illustrious past. In this very place, Cedric reminisced, Harold delivered his immortal answer to the ambassador of the Norwegian invaders. To the rebel Tosti he offered "a brother's love and the fair earldom of Northumberland" in return for peace. But the Norwegian king would get exactly as much as a usurping invader deserved, "seven feet of English ground." (These terms were refused and Harold broke the invasion at the battle of Stamford. But this great victory bore the seeds of Harold's eventual defeat. His army was so weakened from repelling the Norwegians that they were unequal to the Norman invasion that William led ashore a few days later. At the fateful battle of Hastings several days after that landing, Harold and the Saxon way of life perished together.) The stained glass window reminded Cedric of the French craftsmen who had been imported to construct it, and of the countless other ways French culture had been allowed to undermine Saxon England: "We made these strangers our bosom friends, our confidential servants; we borrowed their artists and their arts, and despised the honest simplicity with which our brave ancestors supported themselves." All these reflections on Saxon history were lost on Athelstane, however. The last survivor of the royal Saxon line had only one thought during Cedric's patriotic speech: his appetite. Every pause gave him an opportunity to wonder aloud whether they had been intended to starve (although he alone of the prisoners had eaten upon his arrival at the castle). Cedric finally gave up, with the long overdue observation "that so dull a spirit should be lodged in so fine a body." When the food arrived soon after, Athelstane shot back a bold challenge to Front-de-Boeuf. But the hopes this revived in Cedric's heart faded once more when Anthelstane explained that he would challenge any man if it meant getting out of "a dungeon where they put so much garlic into their pottage (stew or soup)." Perhaps when he is married to Rowena . . ., Cedric ventured, unable to accept the fact of Athelstane's hopelessness as a prospective ruler. Three great horn blasts, as if "blown before an enchanted castle by the destined knight (Gabriel)," interrupted their meal. But despite its apparent urgency they were unable to see what had caused the disturbance.

Comment

Until now Cedric has been unpardonably blind in judging Athelstane. He has overlooked or explained away his oafish character, his stupidity, his selfishness, and his intolerance of inferiors. But locked in a cell with him and the stomach that rules him, Cedric can no longer avoid the obvious truth: Athelstane, for all his pedigree, was never meant to be a king. Scott's management of this scene is broadly comic. Cedric's long-winded and flowery recollection of better days is repeatedly punctured by Athelstane's hunger pains. The old man's intention, of course, is to inspire Athelstane with the glorious history of his race so that he might contribute to its rebirth. But he might as well be speaking to Front-de Boeuf. This is Athelstane's response to the thrilling account of Harold's gallant deeds: "I could have pledged (i.e., toasted) him with all my soul, for my tongue cleaves to my palate." And when the hungry Athelstane directs Cedric's attention to the sunbeams striking the window it has nothing to do with its suggestion of a bygone era; he simply wants to prove that the noon meal is overdue.

This pair of characters, the king-maker and his protégé, reminds us of a similar pair: Fitzurse and Prince John. In both cases the older man, the adviser of a prospective sovereign, finds it almost impossible to operate in the face of his master's faults and vices. The difference is that one of them succeeded despite these apparently insuperable odds.

De Bracy's change of plans is both unexpected and insufficiently defended. How can he hope to win Rowena by revealing himself to her as a common kidnapper? What has happened to change his attitude toward Fitzurse's warning? Is he not powerful enough, as leader of the Free Companions (a band of mercenaries), to discourage any treachery on the Templar's part? One possible explanation is that his change causes a quarrel with his Norman compatriot, which allows Scott to point up the comparative harmony and single-mindedness of the Saxon band that is on its way to destroy them.

Even more peculiar is the Templar's abrupt change of heart. It is true that Scott attempts to account for his attraction to Rebecca in Chapter XXVIII, where he tells us that the necessity of her unveiling before the crowd at Ashby gave the Templar an opportunity to appreciate her beauty. But what then was the purpose of deliberately establishing a link between him and Rowena in Chapter IV? The Templar's burning stare virtually promised Scott's readers that his passion for Rowena could be quenched only by winning her-or dying in the attempt. And the explicit blood-feud between the Templar and Rowena's favorite, Ivanhoe, only serves to reinforce this expectation. Now, without prior development or explanation, he declares his interest in Rebecca. In context, this might be a clever ruse to disarm De Bracy. But as the plot continues to unfold, the Templar's thoughts never return to Rowena, and passion for Rebecca plagues the remainder of his brief career.

CHAPTER TWENTY-TWO

Deep in the dungeons of the castle Isaac awaited his fate, alone but for the skeletons that littered his cell. Now that danger was near at hand he appeared calmer, more resigned than before. After three hours' wait in the darkness, Front-de-Boeuf and the Templar's Saracen slaves entered the room. The gigantic Norman seemed to grow even larger and more ferocious as Isaac shrank before him. Silently he had the slaves set up a pair of scales. "In these very scales shalt thou weigh me out a thousand silver pounds," he said. Isaac was staggered by the demand and swore he owned not a tenth of that amount. But Front-de-Boeuf "had been in Palestine, where, perhaps, he had learnt his lesson of cruelty." His assistants lit a great stove in the center of the room while he explained Isaac's alternative to paying the ransom: "On that warm couch thou shalt lie. . . . One of these slaves shall maintain the fire beneath thee, while the other shall anoint thy wretched limbs with oil, lest the roast should burn." The miserable Jew could hardly believe he was sincere. He pleaded some more, but when the Norman's cruel expression did not change after giving the order to strip him, he could hold out no longer. He would have to beg from his kinsmen, but the money would be paid. Even in this uncompromising position, however, Isaac remembered those who had helped him. He asked that Cedric and his party be released along with him, unaware that he had not been the sole purpose of the abduction. But Front-de-Boeuf disclaimed any control over their fate and demanded to know how Isaac would arrange to pay him. "Let my daughter Rebecca go forth to York" to get it, Isaac suggested. That would be impossible, Front-de-Boeuf replied, somewhat surprised. Thinking Rebecca to be Isaac's concubine, he had given her "to be a handmaiden to Sir Brian de Bois-Guilbert." At this news the old man shrieked and threw himself at the Norman's feet. He offered ten times what Front-de Boeuf asked if only he would deliver her from the Templar. But Front-de-Boeuf had given his word, "nor would I break it for ten Jews and Jewesses to boot." At wits' end and no longer conscious of his own safety, Isaac raged at his tormentor. He refused to pay a penny until Rebecca was released-even if his defiance meant a painful death for him. Front-de-Boeuf, too, was incensed and had all but fed Isaac to the flames when "the sound of a bugle twice winded without the castle." "Unwilling to be found engaged in his hellish occupation," Front-de Boeuf stopped what he was doing and went to discover the cause of the interruption.

Comment

By now Scott's design for relating the situation at Torquilstone is apparent. He has divided the prisoners into four major groups (Cedric and Athelstane, Isaac, Rowena, and Rebecca) and now intends to describe the condition and particular peril of each group in turn. In the first group-Cedric and Athelstane - the only danger was Athelstane's empty gut. Their cell was large and well-lighted, and they suffered no annoyance beyond that of each other's company. In stark contrast, Isaac finds himself alone in a grim torture chamber, confronted by the terrible Front-de-Boeuf. Far from worrying about his appetite, the old Jew has all he can do to imagine the agony the baron has planned for him. He faces the very fires of hell should he refuse to obey him.

Like most of the action dominated by Front-de Boeuf, this scene has the dark, unnatural atmosphere of a Gothic novel (see Chapter XXX for a description of this literary type). Inhuman tortures are inflicted upon the innocent and defenseless by sub-human devils in an infernal setting. Despite these black trials, Isaac emerges from this **episode** considerably higher in our esteem than he has been. He has cracked under the threat of incredible pain, only to retract when he learns of Rebecca's danger. His spirited defiance of Front-de-Boeuf is one of the noblest utterances in the novel: "My daughter is my flesh and blood, dearer to me a thousand times than these limbs which thy cruelty threatens. No silver will I give thee, unless I were to pour it molten down thy avaricious throat." He will risk suffering the worst Front-de-Boeuf can devise rather than tolerate Rebecca's enslavement to the Templar's passions. Nor does Isaac's consideration stop with his daughter. He would also ransom the good Cedric and his party to repay them for the charity they had shown him. Isaac's "passive resistance" to danger (I know of no earlier occurrence of this now familiar expression) also counts in his favor. And for the second time (the first was in Chapter V) Scott pronounces Isaac a fit "study for Rembrandt," reflecting both the author's sympathy for his character and the somber humility of his posture.

The repetition of the same bugle-sound at the end of two consecutive chapters prepares us for another instance of Scott's "reference point" technique. These two chapters and the two that follow them describe four scenes which actually occur simultaneously. The bugle-sound at the end of each helps to synchronize the action of the novel and to suggest certain parallels between the scenes. The first two instances of the technique failed because Scott used them exclusively to bail himself out of a difficult spot in his narrative. Here he is master of the technique, manipulating it deliberately for the purpose of probing his characters more deeply than might otherwise be possible. Like much that is characteristic of Scott's style, his success with this technique is far more impressive than his lapses.

IVANHOE

TEXTUAL ANALYSIS

CHAPTERS 23-28

CHAPTER TWENTY-THREE

The best quarters in the castle had been reserved for Rowena, who was the original object of De Bracy's exploit. De Bracy, dressed in the most elegant fashion of the time, visited her about noontime to plead his cause. For the occasion he spoke in the extravagant **diction** of the courtly lover. She was not his prisoner, whatever the outward appearance of their relationship. Instead, it was he who awaited his doom from her. If he had been excessive in his action it was only for love of the "queen of my heart, and loadstar of my eyes." (A loadstar guides mariners in their navigation.) But Rowena was neither flattered nor moved by his sweet speeches, which seemed so unfamiliar to his lips. With typical Saxon directness she told him to leave such compliments to minstrels and behave like a man, like the outlaw that he was. Stung by his failure, De Bracy accepted her terms. Her choice, he said, was simple: "Thou shalt never leave this castle, or thou shalt leave it as Maurice de Bracy's wife." By this marriage she could leave Cedric's miserable estate and "be raised to high honor and to princely place." Rowena replied that the man she married (hopefully Ivanhoe) would have a higher opinion of "the dwelling and manner in which I have been brought up." The implication did not escape De Bracy, who was well-prepared for it: "Know lady, that this rival (Ivanhoe) is in my power." At first she refused to believe him, to De Bracy's amazement. Had she not known "that Wilfred of Ivanhoe traveled in the litter of the Jew?" Rowena maintained her outward composure at this news and pretended indifference. But when De Bracy threatened to hand Ivanhoe over to Front-de Boeuf, who would have gladly murdered this upstart competitor for his lands, Rowena could control herself no longer. Her accustomed superiority and self-confidence collapsed and she "burst into a passion of uncontrolled vexation and sorrow." Far from encouraging her abductor, however, the sight of such wailing perplexed and softened De Bracy. He could not retreat from the enterprise now that he had revealed himself. Yet her state made it impossible for him to press his advantage. He, therefore, least of the Norman trio, regretted the sound of the horn that required him to break off this interview.

Scott here cites extensive historical evidence of atrocities committed by "those valiant barons, to whose stand against the crown the liberties of England were indebted for their existence" (the **allusion** is to the Magna Carta, executed in the year 1215, by which King John conceded many privileges to his disgruntled but powerful barons). The glamorous myth about liberty-loving English barons is considerably farther from the truth, he maintains, than his own portraits of villains like Front-de-Boeuf and Malvoisin.

Comment

The final piece in Scott's design falls into place in this chapter when Ivanhoe, the hero whom we have not seen since Chapter XII and whose whereabouts have mystified everyone, turns up at Torquilstone. The details of his journey from Ashby and his welfare in the castle are yet to be divulged, but he could hardly be in more danger than on Front-de-Boeuf's home grounds.

CHAPTER TWENTY-FOUR

Rebecca was taken to one of the remoter compartments of the castle, high in a turret. At present it was occupied by a hideous old hag named Urfried. But when the guard attempted to turn her out to make room for the beautiful Jewess, she refused to go. While they went to complain to Front-de-Boeuf of her disobedience, the two women talked. Urfried bitterly warned the frightened Jewess that the same fate she had suffered many years ago probably awaited her now. She was the daughter of the Saxon lord who owned Torquilstone before the Conquest and paid with his blood and that of seven of his sons for a futile attempt to save it when the Normans came. "And ere their blood was dried," she continued, "I had become the prey and scorn of the conquerors." This was the shame that faced Rebecca now. And without a word of comfort or hope for the innocent girl, Urfried left the room. Unlike Rowena, Rebecca was accustomed to fear and danger. The familiar trials of being a Jew had trained her for such emergencies as this. She surveyed her prison and found that escape was impossible. So "in passive fortitude, and in that strong reliance upon Heaven natural to great and generous characters," she prepared for her doom philosophically.

Soon a cloaked figure entered the room. She offered him a rich reward if he would help her to escape, but when he declared in French that her "ransom must be paid by love and beauty" she knew he was no common outlaw, but a cruel and sinister Norman. He was, in fact, Brian de Bois-Guilbert. The cordiality of his initial approach soon wore thin at Rebecca's repeated refusals to yield to him. And when he became more demanding she threatened to denounce him publicly as a renegade Templar who had "sinned with a Jewess" against all his vows. He had only to remind her of what she already knew to answer her threat. Her accusation would never be heard from a sound-proof room. The only hope for her escape was in submitting to him and converting to the Christian faith. But the God of Abraham had provided one desperate escape for his children. As she cursed the Templar ("Craven knight!-forsworn priest!"), she jumped to the window ledge and threatened to kill herself if he persisted in forcing her to his will. Her action inspired the Templar with a new respect for her proud spirit; indeed she was magnificent in her defiance. When at last he had convinced her to return to safe ground, Bois-Guilbert tried to justify his behavior. Love had once been the very core of his life, but the maid he loved and honored married another. Bitterly he sought solace with the Templars; the vengeance and opportunity they offered him compensated for what he had suffered in love. But now that his ambition to become Grand Master of this powerful Order was near success, he "sought but a kindred spirit to share it." Rebecca was to be that spirit. When she reminded him of their religious differences she coldly revealed that the rituals and superstitions of Christianity were mere instruments of his Order's larger policies. Before he could say more, the bugle-sound called him away. Grateful for her relief, Rebecca thanked God for her deliverance from death. But the "wounded Christian . . . one with whose fate hers could have no alliance" also intruded upon her thoughts, despite all the narrow prejudices of her sect.

Comment

In this conflict of wills between Rebecca and the Templar, Scott constructs the last and most interesting of his parallel scenes at Torquilstone. They are parallel, as we have seen, in that each of the last four chapters has dealt with the problems and preoccupations of De Bracy's prisoners up to the moment when a horn-blast announces a shift in the action. Both Saxon "cells" are surprisingly comfortable and spacious. Cedric's was once the Great Hall of the castle and Rowena's, better still, had belonged to the wife of Front-de-Boeuf. But Isaac is thrown into a miserable dungeon, and Rebecca fares only slightly better. Just as Isaac's treatment differed from Cedric's and Athelstane's, so Rebecca's plight contrasts sharply with Rowena's. Although both their adversaries pale beside the menacing Front-de-Boeuf, Bois-Guilbert is certainly more dangerous than De Bracy. A tear is enough to disrupt De Bracy's plans, but it takes a suicide threat to budge Bois-Guilbert. De Bracy offers marriage, at least; Bois-Guilbert, only illicit love. Given such different villains to contend with, Rebecca's courageous faith clearly outshines Rowena's less substantial pride. Rowena crumbles before De Bracy's threats and it is only by accident that her weakness proves to be his undoing as well. Against a brutal and unprincipled demon, however, Rebecca meets the Templar's force with her own inner strength and wins out. On the basis of this chapter, more than any other, Rebecca has earned the admiration of generations of readers, many of whom see little else to value in Scott's work.

One other illuminating contrast to Rebecca is the character of Urfried. She was a proud Saxon beauty-probably much like Rowena-when her home was overrun by the Normans. And doubtless she, too, had Rebecca's choice between a life of shame and a virtuous death (Cedric says as much in Chapter XXVII). But her ugly, wasted person attests both to her choice and to

Scott's opinion of her moral character. Old age can be beautiful in the world of Scott's novels, but only as the reward for a life of virtue: Cedric is the best example in *Ivanhoe*. Later we learn that Urfried (her Saxon name is Ulrica) is Cedric's contemporary, but the striking difference between them denotes the price of corruption and dishonor.

Two further amplifications of the **theme** of prejudice occur in this chapter. Bois-Guilbert's bigotry, which we have long known to be hypocritical, takes another twist or two. Not only does he want a Jewess for a concubine, but the very faith he claims to cherish and defend turns out to be but a stepping-stone for his ambitions. Rebecca, on the other hand, rises one more notch in our esteem by violating the "narrow prejudices" of her own race.* If there were no other explanation of Rebecca's greatness of spirit, it would be enough that she alone among these benighted souls could see beyond the ignorance of her own bias.

CHAPTER TWENTY-FIVE

Summoned by the bugle-call, De Bracy and the Templar met in the Great Hall to discover its source. Shortly Front-de-Boeuf entered with the letter that the horn had heralded. Only the Templar could decipher the Saxon language in which it was written, so he read the curious document aloud. It was signed by Wamba, Gurth, Locksley, and the Black Sluggard, and announced their joint intention to lay a siege to the castle of Torquilstone in the event that Cedric and his fellow travelers were not immediately released from captivity there. De Bracy

* One of the most fascinating ironies about prejudices is that it is not above those who suffer from it most to harbor prejudices of their own.

and the Templar laughed at the impudence and absurdity of such a ragged collection of rascals, threatening to storm a fortress with nothing more than bows and arrows. But Front-de-Boeuf was not amused. He knew the mood of these yeomen for he had felt the sting of their shafts. And when an attendant estimated the force gathered in support of the ultimatum at two hundred men, the master of Torquilstone took little comfort in the thick walls and twenty defenders that stood between him and destruction. Reinforcements were essential. But how to get a message through to York, where all the powerful Norman barons had congregated to pledge their support to Prince John? Front-de-Boeuf conceived a plan. The first step was to send an answer to the attackers. Composed in French, the note declared their refusal to surrender the prisoners. Furthermore, it asked for a priest to hear the confessions of the prisoners, who would be executed "this morning before noon."

This reply was conveyed to the great oak some distance from the castle where Locksley's men were stationed. Here, too, there was some confusion as to who should read the letter, and again the task fell to the only man present who could understand its language, the Black Sluggard. When the shock of Cedric's death warrant receded, the Knight saw a chance of advantage in the request for a priest. Knowledge of the interior defenses of the castle would be invaluable, and no man would be in a better position to carry such information out of the castle than the confessor himself. The Friar appeared to be the only man present suited for the mission, but he had no stomach for religion once he wore his forester's outfit. Fighting was his profession now. The Knight despaired of finding another among the yeomen capable of acting the part of a monk. But when no one else had spoken up, Wamba volunteered himself: "I wore russet (priest's cloth) before I wore motley (jester's cloth), and was bred to be a friar, until a brain-fever came upon me and left me just wit enough to be a fool." With Gurth's recommendation, the Black Knight was satisfied that the jester could do the job. Almost immediately Wamba donned a hooded frock, and with a pious Pax vobiscum (Peace be with you) set out for the castle.

Comment

This is the only scene in which the three major villains of the novel appear together. Scott takes full advantage of the opportunity by developing the distinctions between them that have only been implied in their individual chapters. The primary distinction is between Front-de-Boeuf, whose sole motive in this crime is greed, and his lovesick comrades. Scott acts it out in this chapter by having the lovers appear together discussing the failure of De Bracy's appeal to Rowena, and only then having Front-de-Boeuf join them. It has also become clear that Front-de-Boeuf is easily the most cold-blooded and methodical of the three, with De Bracy at the other extreme of rashness and incompetence. Their different responses to the ultimatum illustrate this distinction quite well. Totally ignorant of the true strength of their defenses, De Bracy laughs uncontrollably with the instinctive snobbery of a sheltered aristocrat who has been threatened by a social inferior. The Templar, less convinced of the immunity of his rank, laughed, "though with more moderation." The only man with his eye on the fact of their danger, Front-de-Boeuf, saw no cause for laughter. In this same vein, De Bracy continues to crow with confidence about their chances; but it is Front-de-Boeuf who comes up with the only concrete plan for getting a message through. For all his villainy, Front-de-Boeuf is the worthiest of the defenders of Torquilstone.

Notes. Aymer's garbled religious stories again work upon De Bracy's impressionable mind. Widespread illiteracy as well as the language barrier are illustrated by the exchange of notes. Wamba's background comes as a surprise, but the association between madness and a religious calling is not new to literature.

CHAPTER TWENTY-SIX

Wamba arrived at Torquilstone and with the help of his all-purpose Pax vobiscus soon ended up within the walls and trembling before Front-de-Boeuf himself. He explained that he was a Franciscan monk who had been apprehended by a band of outlaws to do this errand. He even satisfied the baron's curiosity about the number of besiegers, which had now grown to five hundred. Since he was a stranger, however, Front-de-Boeuf decided not to tell him the message to York but to write it instead. Meanwhile the "priest" was permitted to do his holy office. In a few moments Wamba was with his master and Athelstane in their apartment, and now his real motive for volunteering came out. Once they were alone he urged Cedric to change clothes with him, so that he might walk out of the castle a free man. At first Cedric would agree to the plan only if Athelstane went in his place - "Let the old tree wither so the stately hope of the forest is preserved." But Wamba had no desire to die for anyone but his master, and Athelstane urged the old man to make use of his opportunity. In the end Cedric surrendered. He put on the holy robes, had a brief course in medieval priestcraft ("Pax vobiscum carries you through it all"), and parted tearfully from his friends. He had not gone very far when a woman stopped him and begged, in Latin, for his mercy. Cedric's Latin was quite fresh, but only two words long, neither of which she had uttered. He cursed his ill-luck and hardly heard her plea in behalf of "a wounded prisoner of this castle." When Urfried came to scold the girl, a Jewess, for leaving her cell without permission, Cedric was glad of the opportunity to be rid of her. He ordered her aside so as not to contaminate his "holiness," and Urfried kindly led him out of this predicament into her apartment. Rebecca returned to Ivanhoe's bedside, dismayed that her stratagem had failed. She had persuaded Urfried to let her help with the wounded man, but now a golden opportunity to tell an outsider of their troubles had slipped through her fingers.

Comment

For any who may have thought Cedric's banishment of Ivanhoe a hasty or unnatural act, this chapter provides proof of the depth and sincerity of the patriotic ideals for which he sacrificed his only son. He would gladly have laid down his own life for the sake of the last dream of Saxon glory, Athelstane of Coningsoburgh. Fortunately, as happens so often in this book, the fool has more wisdom than his betters and exercises his right to choose the man who will take his place and go free. It is to Athelstane's credit (as little else in the book is) that he refuses to take the old man's place.

Rebecca again accosts a Saxon from the shadows. This time she impresses us with both her learning (she speaks fluent Latin, a rare talent even among priests) and her persistence in finding ways to help Ivanhoe. The technique Scott uses here of reintroducing a familiar and important character without naming her is still popular with novelists. It is a source of cheap suspense, to be sure, but it also provides a refreshing and realistic shift in point of view. Under the strain of his escape, Cedric is challenged by a girl. She is beautiful, Jewish, and she cares for a wounded man. But Cedric is too frightened to put this knowledge together to identify Rebecca. If Scott were to tell us her name our involvement in Cedric's panic would cease. Scott is not a psychological novelist, by any stretch of the imagination. Cedric does not interest him or us as a case study in fear (compare with Dostoyevsky's *Crime and Punishment*). In fact when Cedric confronts Front-de-Boeuf in the next chapter, Scott specifies that the emotion Cedric feels is not fear (he is trembling) but rage. For the present, however, Cedric is a fugitive bent on escape. And to heighten the interest of this action Scott demonstrates Cedric's momentary fear by his failure to recognize the one Jewess he has good cause to know. Coupled with the **irony** of Cedric's unknowing rejection of his wounded son (through his nurse, Rebecca), this simple scene is a noteworthy sample of Scott's skill in the details of his craft.

It also reveals an important aspect of Scott's conception of the narrative art. For him no character has meaning or significance apart from the actions he performs. Character depends on and is subordinate to the events of the novel. At no time does Scott invent a scene merely to tell us something about a character's state of mind. He may leave the main plot occasionally, but it is usually for the sake of a picturesque description (architecture or landscape), or an irrelevant but interesting bit of background information. Often he digresses to show the reader a strong contrast of character types (the Friar and the Black Knight; Front-de-Boeuf and Ulrica; Locksley and Prince John; Bois-Guilbert and Rebecca; etc.). But even they are what they do, not what they think. An instructive contrast to Scott's treatment of characters may be found in virtually any modern novel. But Robert Louis Stevenson's "Markheim" is easily available, quickly read (it is a short story), and shows how dramatically the writing of romantic fiction changed even in the work of those most influenced by the master.

CHAPTER TWENTY-SEVEN

Urfried had recognized Cedric's Saxon accent and rejoiced at the chance to confess to a priest of her own race. She took him to her apartment and, over his objections, unfolded her history. She was the daughter of Torquil Wolfganger, long believed to have perished with her line when the Normans overwhelmed the castle. Cedric was thunderstruck. Torquil had been his own father's friend and neighbor, and every loyal Saxon remembered the slain defenders of Torquilstone in his prayers. Urfried's guilt was blacker than merely having survived the defense of her castle, however. After the battle she became "the sport of [her] master's passions while [she] had yet beauty," shared his pleasures, and now had been cast away as a worthless slave. Yet she had not been without a measure of vengeance. When hatred between Front-de-Boeuf and his son Reginald (her present master) spilled over, she had the pleasure of seeing the son kill his own father at the dinner table. At first Cedric reproached her for not dying honorably with her family or killing herself at the first opportunity. But when his anger abated he urged her to repent for her sins. Her corruption was so complete, however, that she could not repent. Revenge was the only tonic she wanted. She told Cedric to go out and lead the attack upon the castle, and to press hardest when a red flag appeared flying from the turret. Before Cedric could discover her intention, the voice of Front-de-Boeuf cut their interview short. He was looking for the priest to carry his message of distress. Cedric trembled at the sight of this baron, but more from rage than fear. He accepted the message and agreed (for reasons Front-de-Boeuf could not know) to do what he could to detain the attackers near the castle walls. The Norman was so well-pleased with the "friar" that he gave him a gold coin in advance of the reward that awaited the speedy success of his mission. As soon as Cedric had gone beyond the gates he threw the coin back at Front-de-Boeuf. But a slim hope was better than none, so the baron allowed the "friar" to go his way. Then he ordered that Cedric and Athelstane be brought before him so that he might begin ransom negotiations in case help did not arrive. But when he discovered Wamba in Cedric's clothing he saw both chances for rescue vanish: the "friar" would carry no message and Wamba would earn no ransom. The only remaining hope of avoiding a battle was Athelstane. If they could agree on the terms of his ransom-lifting of the siege in return for his life-Torquilstone could be saved. But Athelstane refused to enter any bargain that did not include the release of both Rowena and Wamba, a price the Normans were unwilling to pay. At this point another visitor to the castle was announced. It was Brother Ambrose, one of Prior Aymer's attendants, who had come to beg Front-de-Boeuf's assistance in freeing the Prior and his company from a band of forest outlaws. Upset by the baron's anger at his untimely request, the priest nearly forgot to mention that the Saxons had built siege platforms and were already attacking the castle. Hurriedly the Normans prepared for their defense. Ambrose was removed to a safer place and Front-de-Boeuf alerted his men for an attack. The Templar meanwhile watched the advancing army and was amazed by their discipline and skillful maneuvers. His suspicion that they must be led by a professional soldier was soon borne out by the appearance of the Black Sluggard among them, his armor gleaming in the sun. For his part, Front-de-Boeuf was glad of the unexpected opportunity to avenge the defeat he suffered at Ashby. As the enemy drew nearer each of the Norman chiefs went to his post to await the shock.

Comment

One unusual sidelight to the Torquilstone siege is that it coincides with the outlaws' attack upon Prior Aymer. The Prior's emissary, Brother Ambrose, bearing a plea for ransom money, could not have arrived at a less opportune moment. Although it may distract from the main action, Scott uses this incident to contrast Norman "chivalry" with the English code of honor.

(We may speak of English rather than Saxon here because Locksley's men do not share Cedric's dream of past glory, nor is their fight so much to revive the past as it is to secure their liberties for a safe and prosperous future. The presence of the Black Knight among them-since he later proves to be of Norman blood-further establishes their integrated, national character.) Earlier Locksley (who never so much as mentions chivalry or Christianity) undertook the rescue of Cedric-a man he had never met-without even being asked and without hope of reward. In the last chapter, Wamba, a dimwitted slave, offered his life in exchange for that of his beloved master-also unasked. But the best Ambrose can get from the "knightly faith and holy charity" of his fellow Normans is an insulting rebuff. They are, of course, under siege and therefore busy with their own defense; but Front-de-Boeuf makes crystal-clear that his deafness to such requests has nothing to do with their present predicament: "When did thy master hear of a Norman baron unbuckling his purse to relieve a churchman, whose bags are ten times as weighty as ours?"

CHAPTER TWENTY-EIGHT

At this point the author must provide his readers with some background to the chapters that are to follow. Rebecca, of course, had prevailed upon her father to assist the wounded Ivanhoe after he had fallen at Ashby. But in surrendering her litter to the knight she exposed herself to the public gaze, and in particular Brian de Bois-Guilbert, who conceived a passion for her on the spot. Jews were the master healers in these dark ages, and Rebecca had learnt her skills well. She knew that Ivanhoe would be better off in her care than with Isaac's servants at Ashby. And since her father had been ordered to attend Prince John at York, she decided that her patient had better make the journey with them. For his part, Isaac consented only when Rebecca argued that he would need a friend if Richard ever returned to power in England. His money had been financing John's conspiracy, and the kind words of a trusted servant of the king (for he knew Ivanhoe to be that) would go far to excuse Isaac's business dealings from any suspicion of treason. Ivanhoe did not reawaken until evening. When he saw the exotic furnishings of Isaac's apartment and the Oriental beauty of his nurse, he thought he was back in Palestine. Rebecca's gentle touch and strange language enchanted him completely. Finally, against her wishes, he started to speak to her-first in Arabic, then in English when she told him where he was. To spare him any embarrassment, however, Rebecca disclosed that she was a Jewess. Immediately the admiration and tenderness in his eyes gave way to "a manner cold, composed, and collected" that expressed only gratitude for "courtesy received from an unexpected quarter." Ivanhoe could not permit himself to regard a Jewess-a daughter of a degraded class-on the same level with other women. He insisted that he inconvenience them no further. Rather than accompany them to York, any Saxon convent or hostel would be good enough for him. But Rebecca told him that she could cure him in eight days-at least three weeks sooner than any Christian leech (healer). And the only reward she asked was that he raise his low opinion of Jews somewhat. Unable to resist such a generous appeal, Ivanhoe agreed to go to York. But first he begged for news of his friends (Cedric and his party) and servant (Gurth), which Rebecca supplied to the best of her knowledge. Once on the road, Isaac speed his train rapidly toward York for fear of outlaws. But soon his lazy Saxon servants began to complain of the pace, and when Isaac questioned the amount of liquor they drank at mealtimes they left altogether. Isaac and his dependents were stranded until Cedric picked them up a short time later. When, shortly afterward, the train was attacked, De Bracy discovered the identity of the man in the litter. Too much a knight to harm a wounded man or betray him to his certain executioner (Front-de-Boeuf), De Bracy kept this secret to himself. But he was also too far committed to the abduction of Rowena to consider liberating her champion and lover. When they all arrived at Torquilstone, De Bracy explained that the litter held one of his men wounded in the forest. The explanation satisfied Front-de-Boeuf, but he assigned Urfried to nurse the patient rather than spare a soldier who would be needed to defend the castle. She, in turn, preoccupied with her thoughts of vengeance, gladly passed the chore along to a willing Rebecca.

Comment

This flashback is awkward and hardly necessary to the progress of the action. What Scott appears to have in mind by this intrusion is a fuller development of Rebecca's relationship with Ivanhoe. Scott describes her skill and delicacy with great affection, and her efforts to mend the sick contrast sharply with the general violence and brutality of the novel. Beyond this we find her combatting prejudice in the two persons closest to her: Isaac, who must be persuaded to help the Christian, and the noble Ivanhoe, who is "too good a Christian" to return the love of a Jewess. In Chapter XXIV we saw the fire in her spirit and the strength of her faith when the Templar tested her; here she demonstrates the wisdom, gentleness and moral courage that complete her as a woman. Rebecca is unquestionably the most desirable character in the novel.

IVANHOE

TEXTUAL ANALYSIS

CHAPTERS 29–34

CHAPTER TWENTY-NINE

As Rebecca watched over her sleeping patient, she forgot the danger of the moment. But when he awoke, the old coldness returned to Ivanhoe's eyes and voice. She chastised herself for doting over this Gentile whose thoughts were only of his father and Rowena. She told him what she knew of their prison, the siege, and added that a priest was somewhere in the castle. On the slim chance that the priest might be able to tell him something, Ivanhoe told his nurse to fetch him. But, as we have seen, her mission failed when Urfried caught her out of the cell. The sounds of preparation for battle rank sublimely throughout the castle. Ivanhoe yearned to take his place in the attack, "to strike . . . but a single blow for our deliverance." But his weakened condition left him unfit even to watch the engagement. To prevent him from opening his wounds in the attempt, Rebecca offered to report the battle as she saw it from the window. The attackers carried no banner, as far as she could tell, but their foremost warrior bore a strange crest upon his shield: a fetterlock and a shacklebolt. First came trumpets announcing the attack and then a deadly hail of arrows from the edge of the forest. With Ivanhoe loudly shouting unheard advice, the Black Knight advanced to the outer walls of the castle, breached them, and cut down Front-de-Boeuf, who was the main defender at that point. Scaling ladders followed up this advantage only to be thrown down. But when the outworks had been won, largely behind the Black Knight's mighty battleaxe, the attackers paused to regroup. Although she marveled at the Black Knight's exploits, Rebecca prayed that God might forgive him the sins of this day. And she chided Ivanhoe for wanting to kill others before his own wounds had healed. The young knight tried to explain the meaning of chivalry and the love of glory to this untutored pagan. Chivalry, he said, was the foundation of true social distinctions among men, the only hope of immortality for frail mortals, the "muse of pure and high affections," and the protector of liberty. But his speech could not blind Rebecca to the human suffering and death that such godless follies inevitably produced. Yes, her people had lost their liberties and their pride for the lack of some of the values Ivanhoe had praised. Perhaps she had no right to judge men at war. Yet Rebecca was hurt by Ivanhoe's suggestion that her criticism reflected "cowardice or meanness of soul." For it was not these things, but weakness that had dispossessed her people. As her patient lapsed again into sleep she fought vainly to keep the Christian out of her mind and heart.

Comment

Edgar Rosenberg (see Bibliography) believes this chapter to contain Scott's most direct statement of the **theme** of this novel: the necessity of compromising unrealistic heroic ideals.

Certainly it is here that chivalry suffers its worst beating. Earlier we have seen Scott pointing ironically to the contrast between the word and the deed of the chivalric ideal. "The Gentle and Joyous Passage of Arms" was in fact a shameful spectacle of human cruelty. In the name of chivalry and courtly love, De Bracy dragged at least five good people to the brink of disaster. Even Richard's crusade was a gigantic testament to the utter failure of chivalry to bring love and religion into the world at swordpoint. But here **irony** is secondary to Rebecca's direct and simple challenge to a code that speaks of liberty and the right but thrives on blood and hate. She is the humane anchor in a world torn between bitter Saxon reactionaries and depraved Norman oppressors. Neither the sad nostalgia of the one nor the bloodstained chivalry of the other will shape the future of England. For in the fanaticism of their beliefs the possibility of tolerance, compromise, and cooperation cannot exist. Ivanhoe, himself a compromise, between Saxon (his breeding) and Norman (his allegiance), is yet the unwitting mouthpiece of the worn-out code. He can see the unreasonable prejudices of his father because he suffers from them. But he is too dedicated to Chivalry to look directly at it and see its flaws. Instead he shouts chivalric **clichés** at Rebecca without stopping to ask himself whether they are true. Ivanhoe, in short, shares with his enemies the vice of narrowmindedness. He is a hero only relatively, because of the lesser degree to which this vice shapes his actions.

Like most great writers who deal with it, Scott's attitude toward war is not easy to define. He obviously endorses Rebecca's pacifism, but there is no mistaking the energy and enthusiasm with which he describes the battle scenes. What does he really think of war? Scott may answer the question himself by having Rebecca describe the battle. She thinks war is evil; yet when she agrees to recite the action for Ivanhoe her excitement is so great that she turns in a vivid and colorful account. Scott may be in the same dilemma. The difference between the character and the novelist, of course, is that he has a choice in the matter.

The technique of describing a battle through the words of a character observing it is not new with Scott. Goethe, the great German poet and near-contemporary of Scott, used it in his early play, Gotz von Berlichingen (1773). Nearly two hundred years before that, Shakespeare (who so often influences Scott) wrote a similar scene into *Julius Caesar*, Act V, Scene 2. But Scott was the first to adapt it to the novel form.

CHAPTER THIRTY

During the lull in the fighting De Bracy learned from the Templar that Front-de-Boeuf had been wounded. He remembered Front-de-Boeuf's angry and impious reply to Ambrose in which he swore that the only help he expected from religion would be the use of a massive statue of St. Christopher to hurl down upon the Saxon invaders' heads. Was his injury a judgment from God? The Templar scoffed at De Bracy's superstition and turned their talk to the defense of the castle. The Saxons had fought fiercely on De Bracy's flank and one of Locksley's arrows had nearly gotten him. The Templar fared even worse, for it was in his part of the fray that the attackers had gained their first foothold on the castle grounds. But when De Bracy proposed that they release the prisoners and end the battle, the other would not hear of it. His pride would not let him surrender to "swineherds, jesters, and the very refuse of mankind." With the remainder of Front-de-Boeuf's soldiers they returned to the battlements and did their best to plug up the weak spots in the castle's inner defenses. Meanwhile Front-de-Boeuf lay alone within the castle, suffering great physical and mental pain. The thought of his approaching doom shook his accustomed contempt for the church, and he wished for a priest to hear his confession. But the godless Templar was the only priest near at hand. Perhaps he should pray? "I dare not," he answered himself. As he uttered these words he heard what he thought to be the voice of a demon, come to torment him with the memory of his sins. "Who stirred up the licentious [Prince] John to war against his greyheaded father-against his generous brother?" But the Baron denied that he had been alone in the crime and defied the demon to punish him for the evil act of fifty men. The voice had not finished with him, however. It reminded him of the blood-stained floors of his own castle. Isaac the Jew? he wondered. Killing an infidel was surely no sin. The "Saxon porkers"? (He is probably referring to the former owners of the castle.) That was an affair of war and honor. Front-de-Boeuf had defended himself on all counts against the "evil angel": "thou seest there is no crevice in my coat of plate - Art thou fled? - art thou silenced?" But there was one more crime to answer for: "No, foul parricide! think of thy father! - think of his death! - think of his banquet room flooded with his gore, and that poured forth by the hand of a son." Even in this he found a loophole: "Go to [Ulrica], she was my temptress, the foul provoker, the more foul rewarder, of the deed." At that moment the voice stepped into view: it was Ulrica herself! She had come to sweeten her revenge at the deathbed of her foe. And as Front-de-Boeuf squirmed in agony before her she unleashed all the poison of her diseased mind. She tormented him with the news of his impending defeat by the Saxon troops, made even more certain by her help. For she had set fire to the castle and in a short while it would crash down upon its defenders. Before Front-de-Boeuf could plead for mercy she had left the chamber and locked the door behind her. His screams went unheard amid the din of battle. As the smoke blinded him and the flames licked close to his body, Front-de-Boeuf, "in the mad frenzy of despair . . . now muttered curses on himself, on mankind, and on Heaven itself." Thinking the echo of his own crazed laughter to be Ulrica's, he cried out for her to speak, "for, only thou or the fiend of hell himself could have laughed at such a moment. Avaunt (either advance or begone) - Avaunt!" But we have looked long enough on the monster's final tortures.

Comment

Front-de-Boeuf's death is a scene straight out of the Gothic melodramas and novels popular for two decades before Scott began to write his novels. The baron and Ulrica are both Gothic types: the dark villain, at war with innocence and piety wherever he may find them; and the beauty he has corrupted and who becomes the agent of his punishment. The torment of Front-de-Boeuf's final moments and hellfires and extreme mental anguish is quite a commonplace conclusion in the Gothic mode. The most famous of these lurid tales was M. G. Lewis's *The Monk* (1796). In addition to having characters of both types that we have mentioned, Lewis contrived an end for his villain that makes the Baron's seem peaceful and blessed. Yet both characters die in an infernal setting, egged on by devils who are waiting to torment their eternal souls. Both have sinned directly against God and man and their blasphemy promises to cost them dearly in the afterlife. When the death of a character coincides with an illusion he has conceived, the reader is always provoked and perplexed. The most famous instance of this in literature, King Lear's final illusion that the dead Cordelia lives, has generated innumerable opinions as to what the playwright intended by it. Is the final illusion in some sense real? Scott has not Shakespeare's suggestiveness, but there is more than a hint that Front-de-Boeuf's illusion may in one sense be real. What he thinks is Ulrica or a "fiend of hell" laughing is in fact his own echo. Thus his last words condemn himself, for if only a fiend "could have laughed at such a moment," he is that fiend.

CHAPTER THIRTY-ONE

Cedric, dressed in the disguise Wamba had given him, made his way to Locksley's band. When he told them of Ulrica's promise to help, they decided to storm the castle as soon as possible. Cedric declined their offer to let him lead the attack, since he was "not a trained soldier in the discipline of wars, or the attack of strongholds." But he was more than ready to follow an accomplished field general. To fill this vacancy, the Black Knight volunteered his experience and skill. He would plan and spearhead the assault, and Locksley would command the archers (a kind of artillery support). On their first attempt (See Chapter XXIX) they took the outworks of the castle, but their position was precarious. They would have to press farther on to the castle grounds across the moat. And it would have to be done before sunset, as the Black Knight could not postpone his urgent business elsewhere another day. Following the Knight's instructions they built a floating bridge to span the moat about the castle, and soon the Knight and Cedric had battled across it and were hammering away at the castle doors. Locksley's archers kept the Norman soldiers' heads down, but the danger to the two heroes remained grave. Above their heads, De Bracy attempted to pry loose a heavy stone from the battlements, large enough to crush anything before the gates. But Locksley kept picking off the men De Bracy ordered to do the job. Just then a red flag appeared on the tower as Ulrica had promised, and Locksley hailed it as the signal of their victory. But the fighting was far from over. De Bracy himself, protected by his heavy armor, had nearly loosened the stone when the Templar approached him and calmly declared: "All is lost, De Bracy, the castle burns." Their only hope now lay in a counterattack that would establish them on the outworks of the castle. De Bracy opened the gates with the intention of throwing back the two men who stood outside, but he underestimated the Black Knight's strength. After a brief and valiant duel, De Bracy was laid low by a glancing blow from the Black Knight's battleaxe. But he gallantly refused to yield until he knew the name of his conqueror. The Knight whispered something into his ear and De Bracy humbly surrendered, "rescue or no rescue." Now a prisoner, he warned the Black Knight of Ivanhoe's presence in the flaming castle and of the danger he faced because of his weakened condition. The Knight rushed to rescue him in the direction De Bracy had indicated. But this was as far as the Norman's help was allowed to go, for the Knight refused to trust him. Dejected and hurt by the Knight's words, De Bracy surrendered his sword and joined the other prisoners. When the smoke alerted Ivanhoe and Rebecca of their peril, she refused to leave the helpless man's side despite his protests: "I will not fly. We will be saved or perish together." But soon the Templar appeared in the door, swept "the terrified maiden" into his arms against her will, and carried her away. Ivanhoe's shouts (which were all he could to protect her) attracted the Black Knight moments later. And as the flames consumed the castle, he carried the stricken man to safety. Everywhere the Saxons were in pursuit of the hated soldiers of Front-de-Boeuf: "The air was filled with groans and clashing of arms - the floors were slippery with the blood of despairing and expiring wretches." Cedric meanwhile liberated Rowena "just as she had abandoned all hope of safety." And Wamba's shouts of victory enabled him and Athelstane to free themselves. These two ran to the courtyard where the Templar, mounted and busily protecting Rebecca from harm, was waiting to escape from the castle. Mistaking the girl for Rowena (despite her black hair), Athelstane threw himself at the Templar in a desperate attempt to rescue her. But the Norman was too much for him and with a single blow severed Athelstane's mace and struck his unprotected head. With this the Templar galloped across the drawbridge to the outworks, where he found De Bracy a prisoner. His late comrade refused to be rescued, but warned that "there are hawks abroad." Escape was possible, he said, only by leaving the country. The Templar thought differently, however, and was certain that "the walls of the Preceptory of Templestowe" would be sanctuary enough. After a hasty farewell, he rode off in that direction with his prize. As the fire in the castle spread and the fighting waned, Ulrica "appeared on a turret in the guise of one of the ancient furies, yelling forth a war-song. . . .the inebriating delight of gratified vengeance contended in her eyes with the fire of insanity; and she brandished the distaff (part of a spinning wheel) which she held in her hand, as if she had been one of the Fatal Sisters, who spin and abridge the thread of human life." As the castle collapsed about her, Ulrica seemed "empress of the conflagration she had raised. At length, with a terrific crash, the whole turret gave way, and she perished in the flames which had consumed her tyrant." After a reverent pause, Locksley led his men in a rousing shout for their triumph over tyranny and designated the place where they would divide their victory spoils the next morning.

Comment

Once the castle has been taken, Scott runs into further problems of plot construction: 1) How to get everyone out of the castle as tidily as possible, and 2) How to prolong his story to fill the three volumes his publisher required of him. There is certainly no good reason for continuing the book beyond this point. The evil Norman barons have been thrashed, Cedric's advocacy of Athelstane has diminished to a point that should allow for reconciliation with his son, both Ivanhoe and the Black Knight have had their moment of glory. All that remains is to reunite the principals and disclose the identity of the Black Knight. To be sure, Ivanhoe and Bois-Guilbert have not had their showdown, but then they never really do. Nor does the budding love interest between Ivanhoe and Rebecca ever develop beyond this point. With the possible exception of the Templar, no character or relationship between characters will change or develop in the remaining twelve chapters of the book. Nevertheless Scott goes on: he lets the Templar escape with Rebecca. This slender and irrelevant digression occupies the last quarter of the novel. The other problem-rescuing the prisoners gracefully-is less crucial, but no better settled. Since the excuse for continuing the story is to be Bois-Guilbert's abduction of Rebecca, someone is going to have to rescue Ivanhoe. No problem here: the Black Knight, a man with obvious but unspecified connections with Ivanhoe, is the natural choice. Rowena? Now we know why Scott has contrived to have Cedric released in the last chapter: he is the only proper person to rescue his ward. Gurth is too lowborn; Athelstane too stupid and ineffectual; and Locksley, perhaps, too attractive. There is no suitable rescuer for Athelstane and Wamba, so they must do it themselves in the most wildly improbable way. Isaac, finally, gets lost entirely in the confusion. No one seems to notice or to care about his absence - no one, that is, but Scott, who reserves a special place for his return in the next chapter.

Two other characters come to a more imaginative end in this chapter. De Bracy, still the chivalrous boob, misjudges the Black Knight as an enemy and walks point blank into a duel with him. He fights well, answers bravely in defeat, and responds respectfully to the Knight's commands (whatever they are). His efforts to save Ivanhoe (echoing Edmund's death-bed repentance in *King Lear*, V, 2) are certainly to his credit. And a man sensitive enough to be hurt by an enemy's unwillingness to trust him cannot be all bad. The most spectacular exit scene in the book is given to Ulrica, the corrupted Saxon hag. In a moment readers would long remember, she chants a primitive Saxon song in her madness and plunges to an eery, terrible, but somehow glorious death amid the ruins of Torquilstone. Thomas Gray's *The Bard* bears a striking resemblance in tone and substance to this scene of Ulrica's death. If Scott was not influenced by this poem he certainly shared Gray's interest in bardic lore and theatrical death-leaps. Charlotte Bronte was one of those who remembered Scott's scene. In fact she duplicated it in the death of the mad Bertha Mason (Mrs. Rochester) in her finest novel, *Jane Eyre* (1847).

Instead of the anticipated recognition or revelation of the Black Knight's identity, the mystery receives another boost in this chapter. What can be the business he must leave to transact? In what capacity did he learn his skill as a military tactician? What can he be to strike such respect and submission into De Bracy's proud soul? Note Scott's obvious repetition of Ivanhoe's whisper to Gurth when we knew him only as "The Palmer." Is it possible that the relation between De Bracy and the Knight is analogous to that between the disguised Ivanhoe and his servant?

One other clue to his identity emerges from the declaration of motives for taking the castle. Cedric, still possessed by his empty dream, wants to "save the royal blood of Alfred" (i.e. Rowena). True to his chivalrous profession, the Black Knight disregards blood and nationality for "the honor of a noble lady." Locksley, perhaps the most sensible of the three (and probably closest to Scott's sentiments), would most prefer to save the gritty little jester, Wamba, who has amply demonstrated his courage and loyalty before them all. Merit is the measure of a man's worth in the forest, not blood or rank.

Scott appears to disapprove of Cedric's unreadiness to take charge of the siege. Little wonder that a man without warcraft has been so helpless to defend the ideals of ancient Saxon civilization. Scott may deplore the ferocity and brutality of knights, but he also seems to believe that a man should acquire the skill to defend his rights and property. Without this a man is, like Cedric, as sleeping dragon-toothless and powerless.

The Templar's abduction of Rebecca is the subject of a famous painting by the French artist, Eugene Delacroix (1798-1863). Besides being a vivid and exciting portrayal of the incident, it is an excellent example of the influence of Scott's romances upon the imagination of artists of his own and the following generation, especially on the Continent.

CHAPTER THIRTY-TWO

It was not until the following morning, at the time and place appointed for dividing the spoils, that the outlaws first noticed the absence of their Friar. Locksley, who presided over the gathering like a king on his throne (for so he was in the forest), dispatched a party of men to search for him in the rubble of Torquilstone. Then he divided the spoils in half and offered Cedric his choice. But the old Saxon was too preoccupied with grief to think of profiting by his ordeal. Athelstane had been killed by the Templar's blow. "A sparkle hath been quenched by his blood," Cedric lamented, "which no human breath can again rekindle." He had delayed leading the funeral train back to Coningsburgh (Athelstane's castle) only long enough to thank Locksley and his men for their help. He also took advantage of the occasion to repay the faithful Wamba for his self-sacrifice and courage. But justice and mercy for Gurth was the only favor the jester asked of his master. Nothing could have pleased Cedric more, for he declared Gurth a free man on the spot and granted him a plot of land to make him independent. Rowena, shaken by her experience but beautiful as ever, next rode forward to express her gratitude. When she had finished and was leaving the "Silvan ampitheater" De Bracy detained her horse and knelt to ask her forgiveness. She forgave him "as a Christian," or not at all, as Wamba observed. Finally Cedric thanked the Black Knight and invited him to visit Rotherwood when he had finished his other "pressing matters of moment." These heartfelt duties done, the Saxons started on their sad journey. Now it was the Black Knight's turn to choose his reward. He asked for and received De Bracy, whom he immediately set at liberty. In addition, Locksley persuaded him to accept the silver bugle from Ashby, to be blown whenever the knight ran into trouble in the great forests. At Locksley's discretion, the remainder of the spoils was distributed among his men "according to their rank and merit," and none disputed the wisdom and fairness of his judgment. Only the "tenth part" of the treasure, allocated to the church, remained to be settled, since the Friar had not yet appeared to claim it. Just as the entire company was about to set out for the castle in search of him, the tipsy Friar stumbled into the clearing dragging the wretched figure of Isaac behind him. He had happened on this unexpected catch while looking for a wine cellar in the castle. When a tower collapsed and sealed them into the cellar together he chose to convert the old heathen rather than die in the company of a disbeliever. By morning, rescuers had dug through to them and found a bag of wine "half-empty, the Jew half dead, and the Friar more than half-exhausted, as he calls it." Isaac swore he had neither been converted, nor promised to surrender all his fortune to the church, as the Friar testified. The "holy clerk" was about to flatten the Jew for his impertinence when the Black Knight stepped between them. Forgetting their past friendship, the Friar struck the good Knight a lusty blow for interfering. To nearly everyone's surprise, the Knight did not budge. And when his return punch sent the Friar sprawling, there was no more argument about the Jew: he would be ransomed like any other prisoner and not harmed in any way.

Otherwise, few of Front-de-Boeuf's men had been captured, but none worthy of ransom. Only one other prisoner seemed likely to yield a profit, "a jolly monk" whose fancy clothes indicated that he was on his way to a "leman" (mistress). It was, of course, "our old friend, Prior Aymer of Jorvaulx," who was next to be led into the clearing for judgment.

Comment

Again the epigraph, or chapter tag, underscores a central **theme** of this and the next chapter: statecraft. Locksley's forest society is a "utopia" (an ideal state where men live together in perfect harmony and plenty). Although they are outlaws and hardly resemble a true society at all (there are no women and children, for example), Scott deliberately likens them to one and Locksley to a popular king. "Pardon my freedom, noble sirs, but in this glade I am monarch - they are my kingdom," Locksley says from his "throne of turf." This "kingdom" has laws and discipline and Locksley is the benevolent but absolute ruler over all. "The Black Knight was not a little surprised to find that men in a state so lawless, were nevertheless among themselves so regularly and equitably governed, and all that he observed added to his opinion of the judgment and justice of their leader." The **irony** of this perfect monarchy is that it contrasts so vividly with the condition of England at that time, victimized and plundered by the treachery and negligence of her leaders. It is no accident, as we shall soon learn, that the Black Knight is the closest student of Locksley's policies and tactics.

Medieval Christianity once more takes a beating in this chapter. Aymer's worldly vanity and the Friar's tippling come as no surprise. But the Friar's unnatural attempt to force Isaac to convert is a characteristic evil of the church, as Scott sees it.

That narrowminded assumption that Catholicism was the only way to serve God was bad enough. What particularly irked Scott was the Catholic's mission to turn others to his way of thinking, whatever the means. There is also a touch of cynicism in Scott's explanation of why several local clergyman agreed to chant a funeral hymn for Athelstane. They do it, he says, "in expectation of the ample donation, or soul-scat" Cedric had promised them. The Catholic notion that money can buy spiritual benefits and privileges is alien to Scott's northern blood.

As in the last chapter, the omission of an important character goes unexplained. We are told that Ivanhoe is safe, but where he is, who is nursing him, and what his condition is, remain obscure. We do not learn until Chapter Forty the answer to any of these questions. On the whole it seems as if Ivanhoe lost his value for Scott as soon as we learned his identity. He has been so much dead weight since his collapse at Ashby and the attempt to reintroduce him later in the book is awkward and unnatural.

CHAPTER THIRTY-THREE

Prior Aymer used all the tactics at this command to persuade the outlaws to release him. first he fumed with indignation at the insult to his holy office; then he laughed in nervous disbelief at the outlaws' threat to hang him; finally he appealed to them as a fellow woodsman. When put to the test of blowing a hunting bugle, however, he hit one fancy French note too many to suit the plain English yeomen. He, like Isaac, would be allowed to leave only after a ransom had been paid. "The lieutenant of the gang" (Alan-a-Dale?) suggested that the two hostages name each other's ransom. Isaac, well-acquainted with the Prior's wealth, proposed six-hundred crowns as a comfortable sum for him to raise, and then offered to lend it to him if he was strapped for ready cash. Aymer in turn set the Jew's ransom at a thousand crowns, a mere fraction of the hoard of gold and silver rumored to be hidden in his house at York. Isaac howled as usual, pleading poverty and asking sympathy for the recent loss of his only daughter. One outlaw, hearing his lament, confirmed Isaac's worst fears: he had seen the Templar escape from the castle with Rebecca. This bitter news softened Locksley somewhat, for he owed the Jews a favor. Back in the days when he called himself Diccon Bend-the-Bow, Locksley had been freed from the gyves (chains) at York and nursed back to health by Rebecca. During his convalescence at Isaac's house he learned where his fortune was hidden, and now he threatened to reveal the secret every time the Jew denied he could afford the ransom. But the memory of Rebecca's kindness, and even Isaac's generosity in giving him a gold coin when he left their house, moved Locksley to help the old man redeem his daughter. First he lowered the ransom figure to five hundred crowns, ostensibly to "avoid the heinous offense of rating a Jew merchant as high as a Christian prelate." As for helping in Rebecca's rescue, his archers would be no match for the mounted Knights of the Temple. He recommended instead a more peaceable course: ransom her from the greedy Templars. For Isaac to get near enough to deal with them he would need a pass, preferably signed by a friend of the order like Prior Aymer. Despite Isaac's pinchpenny interruptions, Locksley bargained with Aymer and got him to write the safe-conduct for a price. When the reluctant Prior complained that he lacked a quill to write the note, the resourceful Captain shot a goose on the wing with "quills enough . . . for a hundred years." Having run out of excuses, Aymer had no alternative but to write the letter to Bois-Guilbert. At Locksley's direction he also scribbled a receipt for the money Isaac was lending him. The Prior's horse and companions were restored to him intact, but the jewels and other finery he had carried with him remained with the outlaws (to spare him the wicked temptation of wearing "the vanities of this life," Locksley explained). Aymer's complaint that the holy objects among these baubles would be defiled in the hands of outlaws led to an exchange of insults with the Friar. Neither, it seems, thought much of the other's priestliness. But they were quickly separated and the Norman allowed to go on his way. Isaac was the next to go. He wrote a note for the amount of his ransom and Aymer's and heard Locksley warn him for the last time to forget thrift while negotiating for his daughter's life. Meanwhile the Black Knight had continued to marvel at the "civil policy" among these outcasts. Now that it was his turn to leave, he clasped hands with the outlaw chief and, although neither had solved the mystery of the other's identity, they parted as true Englishmen and friends.

Comment

Every time Isaac appears, as Edgar Rosenberg notes, he is tagged by his protestations of poverty. Moreover he is usually caught in a dilemma that requires him either to spend money or neglect some human obligation: the gift to Ivanhoe is a conspicuous instance of this. Now his daughter's honor and safety are at stake, but the dilemma persists. He cannot control the lifetime habit of cheapness, so he must haggle even over the price for Rebecca's life. This situation is adapted from Shakespeare's *The Merchant of Venice*, III, i.

CHAPTER THIRTY-FOUR

At York, meanwhile, Prince John and the conspirators who had gathered about him began to worry at the failure of their main supporters to appear. The combined power and talents of Front-de-Boeuf, De Bracy, and Bois-Guilbert were imperative to the success of John's plans. To make matters worse, Isaac the Jew had not supplied the six thousand crowns needed to finance the operation. Before long, rumors of their defeat at Torquilstone began to trickle in, and Fitzurse was forced to report what he knew of De Bracy's escapade to his master. At first John cursed the Saxon troublemakers; then he turned on the barons for deserting him; and finally the blameless Fitzurse felt his wrath for taking too much on himself in checking the rumor out. Just then De Bracy himself arrived to tell the whole story. Both of his comrades were lost, he said, and Torquilstone castle stood no longer. But worst of all king Richard was in England! He had helped the Saxons overwhelm Torquilstone and taken De Bracy prisoner. (We know him, of course, as the Black Knight.) In no time he would gather an army and John's forces would be annihilated. De Bracy and Fitzurse began to talk matter-of-factly about escaping: De Bracy would go to Flanders (Belgium) and Fitzurse hoped a church's gates would keep him safe from Richard. John himself got hold of them in time to forestall a crack-up. Perceiving the unsteadiness of his most trusted aides, he ridiculed their chances of escaping: neither could really hope to evade Richard for very long. Far better to stick out the rebellion and try their utmost to eliminate "this object of our terror" while he was still alone. De Bracy would not harm the man who had just spared his life, however, and no amount of coercion could induce him to lead a party against the king. This time it was Fitzurse who volunteered, after some prodding by his Prince. The Minister turned soldier to prove his loyalty to John and promptly left to prepare for the hazardous expedition. John then assured De Bracy that his refusal to spill a monarch's blood set him higher in the estimation of a man who would be a monarch than a willing assassin like Fitzurse. Surely Fitzurse would obey John's order not to kill the king (no such order had been issued), he said, but if not it would cost him his head. In any case, De Bracy's respect for the crown gave him a clearer title to the office of High Marshal than anyone else had of becoming Chancellor. The two men then went their separate ways: De Bracy to savor the prospect of great preferment despite his hatred for his future king; John to arrange for this "trusted" servant to be followed in the event of his betrayal.

Comment

The second worst-kept secret in the novel is out: the Black Knight is Richard the Lisn-Hearted. Kings in disguise have always fascinated readers, as Scott points out in his *Introduction to Ivanhoe*. From *the Odyssey of Homer* to the simplest folk tales, this basic story has entertained men as long as there has been literature. We are invariably surprised and delighted at the discovery that a noble character is in fact the chief of men, the king. Richard is obviously not a perfect king, however. In the last two chapters we saw the Black Knight studying Locksley's reign and now we know why: Richard himself has never learned to govern. There is much truth to Fitzurse's criticism of his king: "A true knight-errant he, and will wander in wild adventures, trusting the prowess of his single arm . . . while the weighty affairs of his kingdom slumber, and his own safety is endangered." Richard is irresponsible as a ruler, in Scott's opinion, however splendid he may be as a man. We may respect and admire Richard's Lionheart, but this can hardly compensate for the price his country must pay for his private adventures. Only by contrast with the utter corruption and hypocrisy of his brother John, whom we see for the last time in this chapter up to his usual tricks, does Richard seem a desirable ruler.

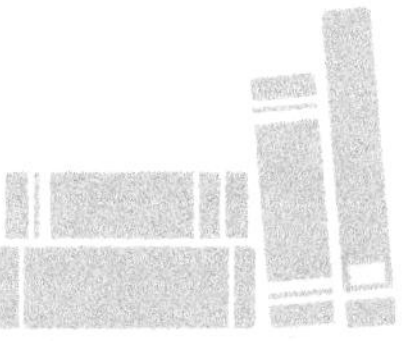

IVANHOE

TEXTUAL ANALYSIS

CHAPTERS 35-39

CHAPTER THIRTY-FIVE

So fatiguing was Isaac's hasty journey to the Templar Preceptory at Templestowe that the old Jew was forced to stop at the house of a friend, Nathan Ben Israel. Nathan at first forbade his guest to proceed on his way. His health was frail to begin with; and Jews were particularly unwelcome at the Preceptory now that they were entertaining their Grand Master. When Isaac explained that his daughter's life was at stake, however, all objections were swept away. With Nathan's blessing, the old man rode to the Templar stronghold. Since the Grand Master's arrival, the usually festive appearance of the place had become somber and austere. In spite of this warning sign Isaac contrived to enter the gates. Inside, Lucas Beaumanoir, the old Grand Master himself, was speaking with his subordinate, Conrade Mont-Fichet, of the moral decay of the English branch of their Order. Although he specifically asked to see the Templar, Isaac soon found himself before Beaumanoir, who demanded to know his business with one of their number. He produced Aymer's "safe-conduct" (unaware of what it contained) by way of explanation, but its effect was not what he had anticipated. The note called on Bois-Guilbert to release Rebecca, but in the most vulgar terms. First, the Prior advised, her presence would only anger Beaumanoir "who careth not a bean for cherry cheeks and black eyes." And the ransom Isaac was willing to pay would suffice to buy "fifty damsels upon safer terms," and the means of forgetting a single bewitching Jewess. Aymer's **allusions** to Rebecca as a "sorceress" and "this second Witch of Endor" (chivalric language for a knight's favorite lady) took on new meaning in the Grand Master's biased mind. Such evil passions, he reasoned, could only have come to Bois-Guilbert through the spell of an evil demon. Rebecca was well-known to have been the pupil of Miriam, a Jewess who was burned at the stake for witchcraft (she was actually a gifted healer of the sick). So she too must be a witch. Isaac's well-meant boasting about Rebecca's powers of curing illness merely substantiated Beaumanoir's theory. She was obviously buying men's immortal souls with unholy remedies for mere bodily ailments. Beaumanoir's course as a militant Christian was clear to him: Rebecca would suffer the same fate as Miriam. Isaac's interview with the Grand Master lasted just long enough for him to hear this terrible doom for his daughter. Before he could plead or negotiate a ransom he was expelled from the Preceptory, and where he had come to preserve Rebecca's "honor, he was now to tremble for her life."

Comment

The next five chapters are set at Templestowe, the last of the four principal pillars of the novel. Returning to his dominant **theme**, Scott uses the Templars (and Beaumanoir especially) as an illustration of the bigotry that arises out of religious fanaticism. The warped logic that leads Beaumanoir, a dedicated and conscientious churchman, to persecute the innocent Rebecca is typical of the worst type of bigot. Rather than admit to an irrational prejudice, such men cloak it behind a "cause" or institution they seem to be defending. The Spanish Inquisition and the Salem witch trials are only the most scandalous examples of bigotry based on ignorance and ending in atrocity. Even Hitler's genocidal attack upon the Jews in our own time was done in the name of a "cause'-Arian supremacy. For Beaumanoir and other fanatics in the medieval Church, any Jew whose customs or skills were beyond the comprehension of churchmen must be in league with demons. This "fact" justified any extreme measure necessary to draw out the evil in them.

CHAPTER THIRTY-SIX

Beaumanoir's next step was to summon the Preceptor of Templestowe, Albert Malvoisin (brother of Philip, one of Prince John's barons). Although no less evil than his brothers in the Order, the Preceptor was quick-witted and cunning enough to conceal it well. When Beaumanoir confronted him with the fact of Rebecca's illicit presence in the Temple, therefore, it took but a moment for him to recover and explain this irregularity. He had known of Bois-Guilbert's infatuation with Rebecca and thought it best to keep them both inside the walls of the Temple where their romance had no chance of prospering. She was here, then, not for the Templar's pleasure but for his reform. This ingenious and unexpected reply-which Malvoisin had concocted on the spot - more than satisfied the Grand Master. It was clear that Bois-Guilbert needed the spiritual strength and guidance of his brethren rather than the lash of their disapproval. But the girl was unquestionably an evil witch. She would be tried before the Order and the public, and sentenced to die. Malvoisin, who would have to justify such an act to the English authorities, objected mildly. But Beaumanoir's contempt for weak English justice was difficult to dispute. Any powerful baron was his own lawmaker, judge, and executioner, he said, and as Grand Master of the Templars he was the equal of any baron. When Malvoisin reported this news to Bois-Guilbert, the knight was smarting from Rebecca's latest refusal of his advances. At first he defied the Order to try her as a sorceress. But his Preceptor had no difficulty in opening the Templar's eyes to the cold facts before them. Any thought of escape, to begin with, was foolish, for the house was full of Beaumanoir's agents. Opposing the Grand Master would, furthermore, mean the end of Bois-Guilbert's bright career in the Order-perhaps even the loss of the Grand Mastership. Once he crossed Beaumanoir, he would be lucky to hire himself out as a mercenary to some petty Belgian price. These arguments at last broke the Templar's resistance. Besides, Rebecca had not made herself worthy of his protection. He said he would agree to whatever Beaumanoir decreed. When Malvoisin left to arrange for the trial, however, the Templar's passions once more overruled his sacred vow. "One effort will I make to save thee," he reconsidered, but "if I am again repulsed, my vengeance shall equal my love." Meantime Malvoisin had encountered Mont-Fichet and was asking him whether the Grand Master was sincere in demanding Rebecca's death. She had done no wrong and evidence against her would be difficult to invent. The issue was larger than a single heathen's guilt or innocence now, Mont-Fichet explained. Bois-Guilbert was too valuable a man to lose over this trifle. And were he to be disgraced by expulsion from the Order, his many friends among the Templars might become disgruntled. No, there was no other way but to make Rebecca the scapegoat-to heap the entire blame upon a worthless Jewess and spare Bois-Guilbert any humiliation. Of course they would need false evidence, so Malvoisin set out to invent all he could. Somewhat later Rebecca was relieved that the footsteps she heard approaching her cell were not the loathsome Templar's. She almost welcomed the guards who had come to escort her to the courtroom. As she solemnly and humbly entered the great hall where the trial was to be held, someone handed her a note. This friendly gesture encouraged her somewhat and she raised her eyes to behold the scene of her judgment.

Comment

The **irony** of Rebecca's persecution deepens as we learn that she will be tried, not for being a witch, but because the Order needs a victim to quell dissension within their ranks. Notice also that a conflict between church and state authority emerges explicitly for the first time here. Apart from the willful barons, the greatest single impediment to national integrity and strength in England was the church and its subsidiaries. Richard must, therefore, reckon with these religious forces as well as the political ones led by his brother, if he is to reassert his leadership.

CHAPTER THIRTY-SEVEN

When the ceremonial hymn opening the trial had ended, Beaumanoir spoke to the assembly. He explained that they had been brought together to rid their Order of a "raging wolf . . . a woman infamous for sortileges (sorcery) and for witcheries." This woman, Rebecca, daughter of Isaac of York, had "maddened the blood, and besotted the brain" of one of their noblest brethren, Brian de Bois-Guilbert. For his part in their crime, Bois-Guilbert deserved to be dismissed from the Order according to their strict regulations. But if this woman was indeed the servant of Satan then their brother's weakness would be easier to forgive. In that event he would receive "only such penance as may purify him for his iniquity"; but the sorceress, if such she was, would pay with her life. The trial began with a number of witnesses who told of Bois-Guilbert's superhuman courage in abducting Rebecca from Torquilstone. Then Malvoisin recalled that he had appeared distracted the night he came to the Preceptory with her. Love seemed to have turned his brain. For his "error" in admitting Rebecca to the house the Preceptor was told to double his prayers and fast for six weeks-leniency made possible by the goodness of his intentions. The next phase of the trial - the investigation of Rebecca's past - was delayed while Preceptor Goodalricke asked Bois-Guilbert what he had to say to the accusations against him. After a pause the Templar offered to answer any charges with his sword, but the Grand Master excused this surly reply since it was plainly the devil speaking through him. The prosecution proceeded to call Higg, a crippled Saxon, who testified that he had lost the use of his limbs while working for Isaac. He was unable to move at all until Rebecca treated him with a miraculous salve. When two "mediciners" said that Rebecca's medicine was unknown to them, it appeared certain to the gathering that there was something mysterious and evil about her skills. Higg asked for the return of his salve when he had done testifying, but Beaumanoir told him it was "better to be bedridden than to accept the benefit of unbelievers' medicine." And when the peasant persisted, he was nearly thrown out of the hall. Now the Grand Master directed that Rebecca remove her veil. When she saw that none would respect or defend her modesty, Rebecca complied rather than allow another to disrobe her. At the sight of her beauty many came to understand Bois-Guilbert's rashness. Higg was moved to remorse for having aided in her conviction, but she forgave him and told him to save himself. Next, two of the Templar's men-at-arms who had been well rehearsed in their parts by Malvoisin were called to give evidence. One told of Rebecca's strange language, clothing, and customs. He swore he had seen her heal a dying man with a few magic words. The other, also embroidering a rumor he had heard at Torquilstone, said she had flown like a bird to escape their master's advances. With this damning evidence the trial ended. Beaumanoir collected the verdicts and asked whether Rebecca had anything to say before she was sentenced. With all the dignity and courage she could muster she denied her guilt and called on Bois-Guilbert to support her. As the audience looked toward the Templar, "agitated by contending passions which almost convulsed his features," he blurted out: "The scroll! The scroll!" While everyone puzzled over his words, Rebecca suddenly remembered the note she had received on entering the hall. Hastily she glanced at it: "Demand a Champion," it read in Arabic. When the Grand Master again asked if she would speak, she was prepared: "I challenge the privilege of trial by combat, and will appear by my champion." But who would defend a condemned Jewess? She could not answer Beaumanoir's question, but threw her glove (gage) to the floor to seal her desperate request.

Comment

Rebecca's piety differs from her persecutors' in much the same way that Christ's differed from the Pharisees'. Her religion consists of love of God and sympathy for the humblest of his creatures; theirs, of superficial obedience to the letter of God's law, regardless of what they carry in their hearts. When Malvoisin stands convicted of poor judgment, Beaumanoir mechanically prescribes the penance that will cleanse his soul. He will say more prayers and eat less meat for a few weeks, and in these empty and superficial gestures God will be satisfied. Beaumanoir makes no mention of repentance, feeling sorry for what he has done-it is enough that Malvoisin observe the forms. Rebecca, too, names the terms of another's forgiveness when

Higg cries out his remorse at having "had a share in murdering her," she, like Christ, serenely lifts the burden of guilt from him with a few gentle and loving words. There are no prayers he must say or duties he must perform, for she has seen into his heart. His words may have condemned her, but his intentions were innocent. He may go his way in peace.

CHAPTER THIRTY-EIGHT

So moved was Beaumanoir by the "simplicity and dignity" of Rebecca's plea that his hardness toward her began to melt. Hardly trusting his own motives, he retracted the sentence of death on the condition that she cast off her heathen beliefs, embrace the teachings of the Church, and enter a convent. But the beautiful Jewess was steadfast in her request. She would not deny the religion of her fathers, and she would have a champion to protect her innocence. At last the Grand Master agreed, unable to fathom the girl's obstinacy. All that remained was to name the knight who would defend the Order. Preceptor Goodalricke picked Bois-Guilbert, and the suggestion was roundly approved. Rebecca, in turn, was advised to find her champion within three days' time or suffer the penalty of death. She regretted the short notice, but put her faith in God's will. Malvoisin meanwhile tried to persuade Bois-Guilbert to take up Rebecca's glove as a sign that he would meet her champion in the lists. When Beaumanoir saw the difficulty he was having and inquired about it, the Preceptor hid the glove in his own coat and accepted in the Templar's name. The court clerk read the sentence, bringing the trial to an end. Now someone would have to inform Rebecca's friends of her condition and need for a champion. No one in the audience volunteered, for fear of appearing to sympathize with the Jewess. Finally Higg stepped out of the crowd and accepted the job. Within a quarter of a mile of the Preceptory he met Isaac, and delivered Rebecca's letter to him. The old Jew, accompanied by Rabbi Ben Samuel, received the scroll from Higg and promptly swooned to the ground when he read it over. The Rabbi revived his friend and then read Rebecca's words aloud. She briefly related her distress and asked that Isaac tell Ivanhoe of her need for a champion. Should he be unable to fight in her behalf, Isaac was to tell him that she died innocent of the charges against her. If God willed her death, her father was to leave "this land of bloodshed and cruelty" for the "less cruel . . . cruelties of the Moors" (in Spain). Isaac arose from his grief to set out after Ivanhoe. The Rabbi, less optimistic about a Christian's good will toward a Jew, rode to York where he hoped gold would buy a defender for Rebecca. Higg waited in vain for a tip for his services, and when it became apparent that they had forgotten him he cursed the Jews and Rebecca for getting him to do their errands for nothing. Yet even in his rage the crippled peasant confessed that he would have done it again for her.

Comment

One interesting illustration of the force of superstition in these dark ages occurs in this chapter and the next. Three characters, independently of one another, find that Rebecca makes them act with unaccustomed generosity and compassion toward her. And all three-Beaumanoir and Higg in this chapter, Bois-Guilbert in the neat-wonder whether there might not therefore be some truth to the charge that she is a sorceress. They are unable to recognize that her beauty and manner have awakened, not evil and corruption, but love in their souls. And so strange is that emotion to them in their profane lives that they attribute it to a supernatural agency.

CHAPTER THIRTY-NINE

That evening as Rebecca prayed in her cell she was visited by the author of her despair, Brian de Bois-Guilbert. He explained that he had planned a different outcome to her trial that afternoon. He had not foreseen that Beaumanoir, with his "silly and fantastic prejudices," would suddenly descend upon the Preceptory and ruin their chance for happiness. Nor had he expected to be chosen the defender of the Order; in fact, he advised her to demand a trial by combat with the intention of appearing himself, "disguised as a roving knight," as her defender. He offered to sacrifice everything that he had ever valued in this life, fame, rank, wealth, power, "if thou wilt say, Bois-Guilbert, I receive thee for my lover." In return for these words he would not appear in the lists; he would renounce the Templars; he would travel to Palestine and make her the queen of an empire there. But at every pause in the Templar's speech Rebecca registered her disgust and contempt for him. If he were truly a Christian knight interested in saving her and not simply in having her for his own, he might easily have requested the help of the king or one of his civil deputies, any of whom would have prevented this injustice. When nothing else could move her, Bois-Guilbert even imagined that life as a wretched, degraded Jew would be better than the guilt he would bear for helping Rebecca to die. His last remark only inspired her to a spunky defense of her people, citing their illustrious descent from "the princes of the house of Jacob." The Templar thought himself truly bewitched when even these words could not overcome his reluctance to leave her. "Thou and I are the blind instruments of some irresistible fatality," he said, tears welling in his eyes. But once again Rebecca corrected him: "Thus do men throw on fate the issue of their own wild passions." His arguments and excuses had run out; now there was time left only for honesty. He admitted all she had said about him, yet "such I must remain-proud, inflexible, and unchanging." At their parting he asked her forgiveness, which she gave "as freely as ever victim forgave her executioner." Even after the Templar had said farewell and left her cell he could not stifle the desire to save her. Malvoisin, to whom he confided these desperate, confused emotions, did all he could to dissuade him. Yet no threat of torture or shame touched the Templar so deeply as the certainty that he would be branded a recreant (traitor), dishonored by his friends, and ridiculed by his enemies. To this argument he at last yielded. His indecisiveness was at an end: "Malvoisin, I will appear in the lists." Wary of his changeability, however, Malvoisin looked to protect his investment in Bois-Guilbert. He had much to gain by Bois-Guilbert's elevation to Grand Master; and Mont-Fichet had implied that he would reward any efforts leading to Rebecca's condemnation. For those stakes he could not afford to trust the Templar's dubious resolution.

Comment

This chapter completes the **exposition** of Bois-Guilbert's character (see Character Sketches). Note that Rebecca's forgiveness of his sins parallels Rowena's of De Bracy in Chapter 32. (Malvoisin emerges as an ecclesiastical Fitzurse in this chapter.) Scott also insists upon her moral righteousness despite the Templar's clever attempts to shift the responsibility for his crimes.

IVANHOE

TEXTUAL ANALYSIS

CHAPTERS 40–44

CHAPTER FORTY

The Black Knight, whom we last saw taking leave of Locksley and his men (Chapter 33), rode to the Priory of St. Botolph's where Wamba and Gurth had taken the wounded Ivanhoe. He spent the night there in conversation with his young friend and in the morning, with Wamba for a guide, went on his way. The two knights agreed to meet at Coningsburgh castle for Athelstane's funeral, where the Black Knight promised he would reunite Ivanhoe with his father. Contrary to the Black Knight's advice, however, Ivanhoe did not wait another day or two to recuperate from his wounds. A foreboding of evil impelled him to leave immediately. He borrowed the Prior's horse, a fifteen-year-old sorrel named Malkin, at the expense of listening to the holy father's advice about her faults and medical history. But it was not long after the Black Knight's departure that Ivanhoe, with Gurth attending him, followed the same trail into the woods. Meanwhile the first two amused themselves with songs as they rode. (Wamba christened them Valor and Folly.) One song raised a dispute over Locksley's outlaws, whom Wamba still refused to trust. After an exchange of puns and quips Wamba asked to borrow the silver bugle Locksley had given the Knight. And when he refused to give it back, the Knight agreed to let him carry it. About then Wamba thought he saw men lurking in the bushes. It was but a moment later that they were attacked by an armed band led by a knight in blue armor. Wamba managed to blow the rescue horn, for the Black Knight was hard-pressed after his horse had been cut out from beneath him. Soon Locksley appeared with some men, relieved the Knight, and easily captured the would-be assassins. The knight in blue turned out to be Waldemar Fitzurse (see Chapter 34). He disclosed the details of Prince John's plot to his king and was granted his life on the condition that he tell no one of the plot and that he leave England forever. Grateful for his timely rescue, the Black Knight revealed himself to Locksley and his band as Richard of England. As they all kneeled, Richard pronounced a general amnesty (pardon) for their crimes and invited them to be law-abiding Englishmen. Locksley responded to the king's secret with one of his own. His real name was Robin Hood of Sherwood Forest-a name famous enough to have reached Richard's ear as far away as the Holy Land. The Friar (popularly known as Friar Tuck) knelt apart from the others, playfully saying his beads to repent his having struck the king. Far from holding a grudge, however, Richard promised to have the good Friar released from the priesthood ("I think it would be best both for the church and thyself") and enlisted as a yeoman of the king's guard. The prospect of so much effort forced him to decline this generous draft, so he received instead Richard's promise of wine, ale, and more than enough venison to help him afford the luxury of sloth. As these glad affairs proceeded, two new horsemen arrived.

Comment

John's plot to assassinate his brother, suspended since Chapter 34, catches us unawares in the form of Fitzurse's ambush. It is difficult to assign a specific function to this **episode** in the development of the tale. It does get rid of Fitzurse and provide an opportunity for Richard to unmask and pardon Locksley's crimes.

CHAPTER FORTY-ONE

Ivanhoe and Gurth arrived on the scene to find the kind standing among "six or seven dead bodies" (his assailants) and a crowd of outlaws. As they advanced, Richard eased the younger knight's perplexity by explaining that Locksley's band had rescued him and now knew his true identity. Satisfied that Locksley was loyal to Richard and the leader of a "company of true English hearts," Ivanhoe scolded his king for endangering his life and the welfare of the kingdom in such foolhardy adventures. But "the wild spirit of chivalry which so often impelled his master upon dangers . . . which it was unpardonable in him to have sought out" prevailed over Ivanhoe's complaints. Richard explained that he had to travel in disguise and without protection to give his allies time to gather their armies, "though his heart acknowledged the justice" of Ivanhoe's charge. A feast of venison - the king's own deer, as Robin Hood reluctantly admitted-was prepared, and everyone shared in the wine, the stories, and the good spirits of the occasion. When the celebration had continued for some time, however, Robin Hood and Ivanhoe began to worry over the king's behavior. First, this delay must hurt his mission - the more critical since the fate of the kingdom hinged upon this man. Second, there was the danger that Richard might take offense at some remark by one of Robin's band, spoken too familiarly in the heat of their carousing to suit a monarch. To avert both of these disasters, Robin and Ivanhoe staged a mock raid on the encampment. A bugler was concealed behind a bush and ordered to blow a Norman battle charge. The blast, of course, brought the revel to an abrupt halt. Richard and the uniformed outlaws rose spoiling for a fight, but Robin said it was just a trick to end the banquet. When his anger subsided, the king admitted the wisdom of moving on and, under the protection of Robin's men, he and Ivanhoe left for Coningsburgh with their attendants. They arrived at the scene of Athelstane's funeral without incident and, as the steward of the castle led the two knights to the tower, they observed the many different groups of mourners, Norman and Saxon, feasting and milling about in the courtyard.

Comment

The hints of Richard's irresponsibility and unfitness as a king that we have observed earlier become explicit in this chapter. He shrugs off Ivanhoe's good advice with flimsy and irrelevant excuses, and finally with the unreasoning force of his authority. Richard's was the "brilliant, but useless character, of a knight of romance" - excellent in a man, but fatal to a ruler. His adventures, therefore, have been fertile ground for balladeers, but not for historians who find "none of those solid benefits to his country" that make a king's reign memorable. Robin Hood, a ruler by merit rather than blood, whose forest regime we along with Richard have come to admire, must stage a fantastic trick (reminiscent of Hal's joke on Falstaff and his henchmen in *Henry IV*, I) to remind Richard of his duties as king. It is with mixed feelings, therefore, that we read the forecast of his untimely death and Prince John's eventful rule: we are sad at the loss of such a splendid hero, but resigned to the fact that such men rarely make history.

Note the impressive and interesting description of the activities at Coningsburgh. Then, as now, funerals had a festive air, and briefly brought together the most divergent and estranged persons to show their common respect for the dead.

CHAPTER FORTY-TWO

As the Steward led them up the steep passage to the chief mourners' chamber, Ivanhoe covered his face to prevent his father from recognizing him. In the room Cedric sat prominently among the elderly Saxon lords whose "downcast and sorrowful looks . . . silence and mournful posture, formed a strong contrast to the levity of the dwellers on the outside of the castle." When the Knight of the Fetterlock (as Cedric knew Richard) entered with his muffled friend, Cedric welcomed them both and led them to the chapel that contained Athelstane's covered bier. Six monks of St. Edmund's convent guarded it, singing hymns continuously to ward off evil spirits. The two knights prayed briefly "for the weal of the departed soul" before Cedric led them to an adjoining chapel. Here the mother of Athelstane, "noble Edith," grieved in solitude. She received them graciously and proudly, and asked Cedric to see to their comfort during their stay. One last formality remained to be observed. One floor above the chapel the fair Rowena led a chorus of Saxon ladies in a dirge for her departed fiancée. Such, at least, was Cedric's understanding; but in fact her grief was due less to Athelstane's death than to the uncertain fate of the wounded Ivanhoe. She alone of the twenty women present retained her dignity on greeting the knights; the others either vainly fretted over their appearance, or scolded those who did. Finally Cedric took them both to a secondary mourners' room and turned to leave. But the Black Knight reminded Cedric of the favor he had promised him in gratitude for his deliverance from Torquilstone. Cedric was somewhat surprised at the occasion the Knight had chosen to claim his reward, but he was glad to grant anything for so noble a deed. The Knight began thus: "When closing the grave on the noble Athelstane, we should deposit therein certain prejudices and hasty opinions." Afraid that the favor would touch upon "the honor of [his] house," Cedric warned the outsider not to meddle in affairs that did not concern him. To prove his direct involvement in the matter of Ivanhoe's banishment, the Knight declared himself to be Richard of England. The old Saxon was surprised but because of his oath (see Chapter 4) could not honor this Norman prince as his king. Nevertheless out of respect for "thy bravery and thy worth" and the boon (reward) he had promised Richard, Cedric forgave his son. There were two conditions to their reconciliation: first, Ivanhoe would have to give up the frills and fashions of Norman court life in favor of the plain, functional English styles of his ancestors; second, Rowena could be his only after she had mourned Athelstane for two full years. There was no time for rejoicing, however, for no sooner had his name been spoken than the "dead" man, Athelstane himself, burst into the room, "pale, haggard, and like something arisen from the dead!" When he had caught his breath and Cedric had plucked up enough courage to address him, Athelstane told a harrowing tale of his last three days. The Templar's blow during the fighting at Torquilstone had only stunned him, although he appeared quite dead. When he awoke that night on the altar of St. Edmund's he was too groggy to surmise what had happened to him. He asked for wine to clear his head, but the monks (who expected to profit handsomely by his dead) fed him a sleeping potion in the hope of concealing the news of his recovery. Since then he had suffered every sort of terror and abuse at their hands (especially directed at his appetite) before he was able to escape from St. Edmund's and return to his own castle. As Athelstane spoke, Cedric's faded dream of Saxon glory began to revive. When the strange tale was ended and Athelstane has sworn to punish the treacherous priests, Cedric called on him as "a male descendant of the Holy Confessor" to challenge Richard's right to the throne of England. But Athelstane's experience had purged his flagging ambitions. He renounced his claim to the crown and swore allegiance to Richard; more than that, he surrendered Rowena to Ivanhoe since "she loves the little finger of my kinsman Wilfred's glove better than my whole person." When he turned to congratulate Ivanhoe, however, he was nowhere to be found; nor was Rowena in the room; nor even the King into whose service he had just pledged himself. Ivanhoe, it was later learned, had left hurriedly after speaking with a Jew; and Richard, hearing this, questioned the same Jew and followed on the heels of his young liege-knight. Thus mysteriously bereft of his mourners, Athelstane concluded that the castle was haunted, and hastened to dinner lest that vanish as well.

Comment

Athelstane's return from the dead was so fantastic that Scott added a footnote to the 1830 edition of his novels, apologizing for it and blaming his editor for the suggestion. But the damage had been done and Scott chose not to rewrite the chapter. Since then this blemish has provided many of Scott's critics with a solid complaint against his taste and craftsmanship. Absurd though it is, Scott seems to have been quite aware of what he was doing. For instead of playing the scene straight he turns Athelstane's "resuscitation" into a hilarious farce. The very image of this oaf dressed in his burial clothes, a terrifying sight at first, becomes quite ridiculous as the shock wears off. We recognize the same old Athelstane as soon as he begins to describe the ravages to his diet. His sensible release of Rowena from their engagement reminds us of many another unwanted suitor in comedy (Tony Lumpkin in Goldsmith's *She Stoops to Conquer* is a close relative). And his triple-take at the end of the chapter, in which the three persons he addresses in succession turn out not to be there, is sheer fun. Scott's treatment of this subject should be compared with a more conventional tale of walking dead, like Poe's "Fall of the House of Usher." Scott's humor is often strained, but here the wry tone of his narrative suggests that he credits this part as little as we do, and that, despite superficial resemblances to the Gothic novelists, he was not prepared to take their mood quite seriously.

Athelstane's return also permits Scott to adorn his story with a couple of literary quotations. When Athelstane drops in on Cedric and the two knights, the old man addresses him in much the same language and tone that Horatio uses in speaking to Hamlet's ghost. And Scott's reading of Italian literature apparently did not end with Ariosto, for the story of evil monks trying to persuade a simple-minded sinner that he is in Purgatory appears in Boccaccio's *Decameron* (Third Day, Eighth Story).

Oddly enough, the dismal implications of Athelstane's death are in no way brightened by his return. In a real sense, the old men who mourn him are a "band of ancient worshippers of Woden called to life to mourn over the decay of their national glory." For whether Athelstane lives or not, these men are relics of a dead civilization. Athelstane's repudiation of his title to the throne merely confirms an already obvious fact. Saxons must now join with Normans (as they do in the courtyard outside the mourning chambers) in forging an English nation, at the cost of their racial identity. Cedric and those like him will never understand or accept this but it is only a matter of time before their sad memories and futile hopes will pass away. And with them will pass one more source of the bigotry that has kept England divided and weak.

CHAPTER FORTY-THREE

A great crowd had gathered outside the Preceptory to witness Rebecca's trial by combat. At one end of the lists stood the Grand Master's throne; and opposite was the execution stake piled round with wood, where Rebecca would be burned to death if her champion failed to appear. As the people waited for the parade of Templars to emerge from the castle, the rumor of Athelstane's awakening from his death-sleep circulated among them. Alan-a-Dale, a minstrel (and one of Robin Hood's lieutenants). perceived the interest of his friend and companion, Friar Tuck, in the story; and soon he got the stout priest to admit having witnessed Athelstane's miraculous recovery while visiting St. Edmund's convent. In fact, the terror of seeing the dead man reappear had impelled the Friar to attend "some good work such as the burning of a witch," which explained his presence at the Templar ceremony. Now the procession began: first the members of the Order and then the condemned woman. Rebecca, full of "courage and resignation," was seated near the stake to contemplate the grim prospect that confronted her. Meanwhile the Grand Master received the assurances of Preceptor Malvoisin that Bois-Guilbert had sworn the mandatory oath "that his quarrel is just and honorable" - a lie that Malvoisin thought justified by his interest in the Templar's fortunes. Now the call for a champion to defend the prisoner was sounded. After some minutes no one had appeared to answer for her. Beaumanoir agreed to give her until noon to produce a defender, but at that time she would be committed to the flames. One last time Bois-Guilbert, his face contorted with conflicting passion, offered to save Rebecca in return for her love. But her answer was the same. Just as her two-hour reprieve had ended and a murmur of expectation arose from the crowd, a lone rider appeared in the distance. But the hope this sight aroused in Rebecca's breast dimmed when the knight entered the lists. For he was exhausted and kept his saddle only with difficulty. He nevertheless announced his intentions, as Wilfred of Ivanhoe, to defend Rebecca's honor. Even Bois-Guilbert regretted his weakened condition, but when the Templar told him to rest up and get a fresh horse, Ivanhoe refused. He reminded Bois-Guilbert of their appointment to fight to the death, and demanded that he keep it now or take the name of coward. The proud Templar hotly accepted the challenge and, when the Grand Master and Rebecca had approved their defenders, the two knights rode to either end of the lists and charged. As expected, it was the knight of Ivanhoe who fell to the ground after their first collision, and who now rose, sword in hand, to engage the stronger man. But the Templar had also fallen, although only grazed by Ivanhoe's lance. He would not rise again, for he was dead, "a victim of the violence of his own contending passions." God's will had been done, and his verdict was that Rebecca go free.

Comment

Alexander Welsh observes that Scott's conventional heroes never kill their enemies, since this would disqualify them for the rewards of the gentleman's life that Scott glorifies in his novels. It is apparently with this notion in mind that Scott strains the credibility of his readers by having the Templar die from natural causes (a heart attack, probably) at the instant of his clash with Ivanhoe. One excellent critic of Scott's novels seriously maintains that this **episode** is the magnificent tragic **climax** of the story (C. A. Young). Whatever Scott intended by it, for sheer improbability this scene ranks a mere shade behind Athelstane's recovery in the previous chapter. It also reminds us of Scott's detestation of senseless and unnecessary violence. He has expressed this feeling in the Ashby and Torquilstone incidents, and here again Scott compares the bloodthirsty audience to modern crowds that gather to watch "an execution, a bruising match, a meeting of radical reformers" just for the pleasure of watching "brave men falling by each other's hands."

Once more Normans and Saxons are wedded by the anti-Semitism they share (as in Cedric's hall). But twice Rebecca's beauty evokes sympathy from "the most hardened bigot" in the mob. Just as the prejudices of individual characters has been eroded or modified in the course of the novel, so the "prepossessions and prejudices of the multitude" have also subsided. Scott is hardly optimistic about the human tendency towards discrimination, but some progress is evident in the book.

CHAPTER FORTY-FOUR

As the Grand Master was proclaiming Ivanhoe the victor, King Richard rode into the lists at the head of an armed company of knights and soldiers. He scolded Ivanhoe for his rashness in leaving Coningsburgh and spoke a brief eulogy upon seeing the Templar's dead body. But the chief business of his visit was to arrest Malvoisin as a traitor and to disband the Templar company at Templestowe. Beaumanoir was furious and threatened reprisals against the English throne for this "usurpation" of church property and privilege. But Richard had made up his mind and ordered the Grand Master and his followers to find less treasonable headquarters. At first it seemed as if the Templars would fight for their rights, heartened as they were by their leader's proud defiance of the king. But when none accepted Richard's challenge to cross lances with him, the Grand Master declared that his men would have no part in earthly quarrels and led them away in a huff. Rebecca was comforted by her father during these proceedings. When she regained her senses she asked to be taken away without a word to Ivanhoe. Isaac thought this ungrateful, but she had only to remind him that King Richard would deal harshly with the treasurer of John's conspiracy, Isaac himself, if they lingered. Together they stole away from the lists, unnoticed by any of the company. Ivanhoe was relieved that the king had shown enough prudence to bring an armed guard with him to the enemy's stronghold. But the Earl of Essex, one of Richard's party, corrected the knight's error. He and his men had intercepted Richard in the forest entirely by chance. It was all they could do to prevail upon him to accept their assistance.

Prince John's revolt was soon put down and most of its leaders punished: the Malvoisins were executed, Front-de-Boeuf was already dead, and De Bracy and Fitzurse had fled the country. But John himself "was not even censured by his good-natured brother." Cedric's dream of a Saxon king soon followed John's conspiracy to the scrapheap. Rowena, of course, loathed Athelstane, and he became so involved in his revenge against the church that he had no thought for her. An alliance between them was quite out of the question. And as Cedric's obstinacy and hatred for Normans began to soften, he approved his son's marriage to the beautiful Rowena. Their wedding was splendid, and the king himself attended. Norman and Saxon aristocrats joined together in celebrating the wedding "that marked the marriage of two individuals as a pledge of the future peace and harmony betwixt two races, which, since that period, have been so completely mingled, that the distinction has become wholly invisible." Although it was many years before a single English language emerged to replace its Norman and Saxon ancestors, integration of the two races was evident even in Cedric's lifetime. Two days after the wedding Rebecca visited the bride to "pay the debt of gratitude" she owed Ivanhoe. She said that she would go to Spain with her father, for England was a "land of war and blood surrounded by hostile neighbors, and distracted by internal factions . . . on safe abode for the children of my people." Rowena's attempts to change her mind failed. In parting, the Jewess asked to see Rowena's face, in which she found "a tinge of the world's pride or vanities" mixed with gentleness and goodness well-suited to her "noble deliverer." Tearfully she gave Rowena a box of jewels, a last token of affection. They would be of no use to her in the future for she had chosen to devote her life to "tending the sick, feeding the hungry, and relieving the distressed." After Rebecca had gone, Rowena told her husband of the interview. And in the years that followed Ivanhoe recalled "Rebecca's beauty and magnanimity" more often than Rowena might have liked. As to his public career, "Ivanhoe distinguished himself in Richard's service" until the king's untimely death in France some years later.

Comment

If this novel were a simple-minded romance, aimed only at pleasing and diverting its readers, its conclusion would certainly be a disappointment to them and a miscalculation on the author's part. Romances are expected to end happily. The lovers should be paired off with perfect mates, and a rosy future should await all the sympathetic characters in the story. In that way we might have put down this book glowing with satisfaction at having visited a world far better than our own. There is no question that, on the surface, Ivanhoe does promote this feeling. The future of England has been secured by the return of its strong enlightened monarch. Richard, by displacing the Templars and suppressing John's plot, has established the clear superiority of the crown over the church and other dissident elements in the state in matters of civil law and authority. Through Richard's continuous efforts to ingrain tolerance in his people, Norman and Saxon factionalism is nearing its end. Prejudice and bigotry, racial and religious, appears unlikely to survive this generation of Englishmen. And the marriage between Rowena and Ivanhoe is a symbolic celebration of these great achievements of Richard's reign. For by helping the lovers surmount Cedric's prejudice, the king has done, on a personal level, much the same thing that he has done for the nation as a whole. But two clouds remain to threaten this blissful state of affairs. The first is Rebecca. Her decision not to thank Ivanhoe after his joust with Bois-Guilbert probably saved her from a dull marriage to a man unequal to her. It is not, therefore, her failure to marry well that distresses us so much as her reasons for leaving England. In the first place, of course, she wants to remove herself far from the man she loves and has now lost. But the explanation she gives Rowena is probably more to Scott's point.

Notwithstanding all that has happened since the opening of the novel, England is still unready to receive and preserve its saints. The gentlest and noblest of human kind is driven to seek her peace and welfare in a land of infidels: Moorish Spain. Rebecca's departure, then, is a telling commentary on the moral sickness of medieval England and an ominous forecast of future woes. Even more telling, since it is a statement of historical fact, is Scott's final word in the novel. With the many references to Richard's inadequacies as king in the back of our minds, we read that his reign will come to an abrupt end, and with it all the bright hopes for our hero's future. True, the book ends peacefully and in joy. All the important conflicts have been settled, and nearly everyone we are expected to care about is well-off. But Scott is too much of a realist to put a "happily-ever-after" tag on his story. For as long as ignorance plagues the human condition-whether in chivalric daydreams or in the nightmares of bigots - no happy ending can be a final one.

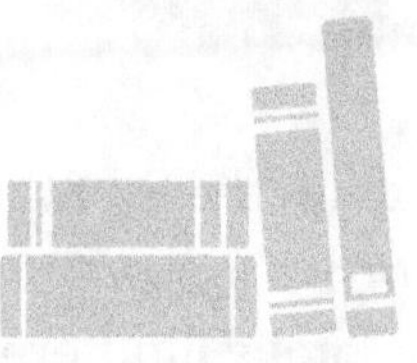

IVANHOE

CHARACTER ANALYSES

Of the sixty-odd speaking characters in *Ivanhoe* the twenty sketched below are the most prominent. They are grouped according to race (Saxon, Norman, and Jew), and listed in order of their social rank. A possible source of confusion in a first reading of *Ivanhoe* is the profusion of nicknames and aliases by which these characters may be known. Each is referred to by the name Scott uses most often, with secondary names and titles in parentheses.

SAXONS

Athelstane Of Coningsburgh (The Unready)

As the only living descendant of the royal line of Edward the Confessor, last undisputed Saxon king, Athelstane is the only hope for a Saxon resurgence. Ironically, few men have ever been so unequal to a great task, so lacking in the ingredients of greatness, as Athelstane the Unready. The blindness of Cedric's prejudice and the futility of his dream of Saxon glory are made quite explicit by the incompetence of the man he pins his hopes on. Athelstane is stubborn, clumsy, coarse, lazy, and vindictive, not to speak of his being totally indifferent to the future of Saxon culture and government. His only motive in allowing Cedric to make him king is a lukewarm ambition to be raised above better men. For the most part a harmless fool, he is a butt for much of the novel's humor with his ravenous appetite and dull brain.

Rowena

Beautiful descendant of the royal line of Alfred the Great, ninth century Saxon king and one of the heroes of English history. Ward of Cedric the Saxon, understood to be the fiancée of Athelstane, but in love with Ivanhoe. For love of her, Ivanhoe has been disowned and now returns to face incredible dangers. The mere sight of her fires the Templar with passion. Prince John thinks her so beautiful and noble as to deserve a Norman husband; and De Bracy becomes so excited at the prospect of having her that he engineers a crude abduction that brings on the siege of Torquilstone. Athelstane nearly gets himself killed-twice-for her sake. And Rebecca abandons her own chance of happiness with Ivanhoe by stepping aside for the more "suitable" Rowena. Why all the fuss? Scott tells us she is beautiful-even describes her. But somehow we do not feel her beauty. She is too reserved, distant, and imperial to appeal to modern readers-too perfect and uninteresting. Scott says she is proud and pious and noble and generous, but each time all we see is the same pretty but expressionless figure going through the same stiff motions as before. Perhaps any conventional female must pale beside Rebecca, but Rowena is the one whose doom if became to set off the brilliance of the magnificent Jewess.

Cedric Of Rotherwood (The Saxon)

Owner of the great estate of Brotherhood and a Saxon leader, although not of royal blood. Father of Ivanhoe, guardian of Rowena, and self-appointed protector of the fast-fading Saxon way of life. Cedric bears a striking resemblance to Shakespeare's *King Lear*. Each is the ruler of his realm (a nation in Lear's case, a manor in Cedric's) - an old man, strong-minded, proud, irritable, and magnanimous. Neither has the comfort of a wife (in fact none is ever mentioned), and they are troubled by the lack of a male heir (Cedric, remember, had disowned Ivanhoe). They both cling to a vision of faded glory: Lear's, that he is still (at eighty years of age) the titan of a man he once was; Cedric's, that the dying Saxon civilization will somebody thrive again. Each rashly disowns a loyal and loving child, and promotes an unworthy substitute. As the repercussions of this fatal mistake begin to torment them, each is attended and comforted by two servants: a faithful retainer who returns to save his master even after suffering injustice at his hands; and a fool whose pointed wit packs more wisdom than folly. Both these servants see the error of their master's ways and do their best to set him right. The trials and discoveries which follow include the return of the disinherited child to fight on behalf of the father, and their subsequent imprisonment together. Near the end of the story the father sees his mistake and is reconciled with his child. Unfortunately Cedric lacks the size, the power, and the pathos that raised Shakespeare's tragic hero above mere senility. Unlike Lear, Cedric is bumbling and ridiculous in his obstinacy. Nothing he does earns our sympathy or respect; even the reconciliation with Ivanhoe seems to be done grudgingly. Both men are dying remnants of a past generation, but Lear explodes brilliantly on his exit where Cedric merely dodders toward an overdue grave.

Wilfred Of Ivanhoe (The Palmer, The Disinherited Knight, Desdichado)

One of Richard's elite troop of English knights during the Third Crusade, he is also a dedicated son and a gallant lover-a noble young man without stain. Like Rowena he is blond, blue-eyed, handsome, and well-formed. Indeed he is so perfect that Scott himself seems to have lost interest in him after Chapter 12. Up to that point the mystery of his identity had held our curiosity fairly well. But once that is cleared up, Scott offers nothing else to sustain a reader's interest in Ivanhoe. To be sure, he shows up again at Torquilstone and flirts a bit with Rebecca, but by then Scott is far more involved with the effect of a hopeless love on Rebecca than in the stodgy prejudice of his "hero." And the last few chapters, when Ivanhoe once again figures prominently, are spent tying up loose ends, arranging for everyone's happiness and well-being, and for this he can hardly be spared. Thematically, Ivanhoe is more interesting than as a character. The central conflicts of his story begin and end with bigotry: Bois-Guilbert hates him for being a Saxon, and his father disowns him for his Norman connections. But Ivanhoe can also be prejudiced, as in his scorn for Isaac and especially his rejection of Rebecca. In neither instance, however, does his cruelty match that of his countrymen; and both times he repairs the injury with a noble act. If only by default, then, Ivanhoe is the most tolerant character in the Novel (Rebecca and Richard excepted). When we add to this that he represents the best of both Norman and Saxon cultures, his significance is incontestible, however dull he may be personally.

Urfried (Ulrica Torquil)

Daughter of Wolfgang Torquil, a great Saxon lord, she was long thought to have perished with her father and brothers in the unsuccessful defense of their castle against Norman invaders (led by Front-de-Boeuf's father). Instead she has lived concealed as the baron's concubine (and later his son's) until, her youth and beauty spent, she is cast aside and reduced to a serving woman. In the wake of this sin and humiliation her mind snaps and she wreaks a terrible revenge on Front-de-Boeuf during Locksley's siege of the castle. As she awaits death high amid the flames consuming Torquilstone, she sings a primitive Saxon chant revealing the passionate, barbaric roots of her bloody crimes. Between them, Athelstane and Ulrica stand for all that is corrupt and backward in Saxon culture. Their presence in the novel does much to dispel the common impression that Scott is prejudiced in favor of the oppressed Saxons.

Locksley (The Yeoman, The Captain, Robin Hood, Diccon Bend-the-Bow)

One of the most exciting figures in the novel, Locksley is only dimly realized as a character. We have no interest in him as an individual because he is self-sufficient and superb in whatever he does, from archery to ruling a kingdom. He is in love with no one, makes no mistakes, performs generous acts of daring, and appears to speak wisely every time he opens his mouth. (His prejudice against Jews is of the same order as Ivanhoe's.) What purpose does such perfection serve? First, it is appropriate to the mythical aspect of a hero of English folklore. He is, like his namesake Robin Goodfellow (Puck of Shakespeare's *Midsummer Night's Dream*), the resident genius (indwelling spirit) of the forest. There he is king, the master over life and death who sees and knows all and who deals with trespassers (like De Bracy and his gang) at his discretion. (See comment on Chapter 32 for discussion of the importance of his "reign" to the larger **themes** of novel.) In this capacity he rules his forest with wisdom and in peace, policies his precinct, and rescues Cedric. Then there is his historical aspect as the bowman and bandit of old English ballads. In this role he performs amazing feats of skill at the archery contest, treats Gurth with fairness and mercy at Ashby, and reveals a noble heart entirely out of keeping with his profession.

Friar Tuck (Friar Of Copmanhurst)

Saxon monk (a hermit) and "spiritual father" to Robin Hood's outlaw band. He is a lusty, down-to-earth, life-loving man who helps God's work along with a broadsword and quarter-staff when prayer fails. He believes that formal religion is for those who can afford the freedom and leisure it requires. When these are scarce among his flock, a holy man's place is at the head of their struggle to regain them. In this secular tendency he resembles a Protestant minister of Scott's own time more than a medieval monk. (Aymer is a truer representative of the decadent clergy at the end of the Middle Ages.) For all this, Friar Tuck is still a hypocrite and an opportunist in the tradition of Falstaff. He is enormously fat, an engaging and willing drinking companion, and an accomplished thief. He can trade in insults and blows with almost any man. But he can be cruel and stupid, as in his mistreatment of Isaac. Unlike Falstaff, there is no question of the Friar's courage, if we except his refusal to enter Torquilstone as a spy. Yet both are characters who charm us in spite of their vices.

Gurth

Cedric's loyal swineherd who, like Eumaeus in Homer's *Odyssey*, is the first to recognize his master (Ivanhoe) when he returns home from the wars in disguise. Gurth is primarily a slave, judging by Scott's interest in the collar he wears. He is earthy, "surly," superstitious, but capable of uncommon fidelity. Instead of intelligence he has inborn common sense and shrewdness; and his stubborn defiance of the Normans who cross his path reveals fierce national pride, despite his class. When we meet him he stands for all that is characteristic of the Saxon race-a base-born Cedric. Yet he is a perfect straight-man for Wamba's jests, which are usually out of reach of his uncultivated mind. We are disappointed at his failure to defend himself to Cedric (Wamba must do that). But when Ivanhoe makes him his squire and entrusts him with the errand to Isaac, our confidence in him is restored. His joust with the Miller is one of the comic high-points of the novel. Even more significant than his service to Ivanhoe is the way he responds to Cedric's injustices. He is like his dog, Fangs, who returns good for evil, service for slight. Even after Cedric has put him in irons and wounded Fangs, Gurth risks his life to save his master. Gurth's reward for his dutiful and courageous conduct is the freedom that has been his dream since his first appearance in the novel. Then he cursed the hardships of Norman tyranny, but now he has earned his release from bondage to Cedric or any other man, as well. Gurth is an ancestor of the English working classes whose struggle for freedom challenged the peace of Scott's own time.

Wamba

Slave and jester to Cedric the Saxon. Like the fool in *King Lear*, he has all the virtues of his simplemindedness. He is unswervingly loyal to his master. When Gurth is freed late in the novel as a reward for his bravery, Wamba speaks for the opposite point of view. He would rather have the comfort and protection of a kindly master than face the responsibilities of total independence. This is a direct reflection of his love for Cedric, as well as a fairly sophisticated bit of philosophy. Except for his distrust of the outlaws, Wamba's wisdom is as noteworthy as his loyalty. It is the wisdom of a mind uncluttered with the emotions and problems of common men. Wamba has no self-interest, no ambition, no passion to cloud his access to truth. Frequently, therefore, his asides make more sense more clearly than the lengthy speeches of his superiors. And because of his affection he can speak out honestly without fear of reprisal. His courage, however, is his dominant trait. He stands up to both Bois-Guilbert and Cedric, when he knows he is in the right. He alone fights well during the ambush of Cedric's train, and later he brazens his way into Torquilstone and swaps his life for Cedric's. When he and King Richard become traveling companions toward the end of the book, the apparent disparity of their rank is lost beside the fact that they are the bravest figures in a world of heroes. Unfortunately, Wamba's wit falls short of Scott's pretensions for it. His jests are either too broad or too learned for our amusement. In general, however, Scott's estimation of him and ours is summed up in Locksley's tribute. "Were there no other cause [for storming Torquilstone] than the safety of that poor faithful knave, Wamba, I would jeopard a joint [i.e. "risk my neck"] ere a hair of his head were hurt."

NORMANS

Richard I Of England

(Richard the Lion-hearted, Coeur-de-Lion, Richard of Anjou, Richard Plantagenet, the Black Knight, the Black Sluggard, Le Noir Faineant, Knight of the Fetterlock and Shacklebolt): In Richard the skill and temperament of an incomparable knighterrant clash with his responsibility as the king of a young and troubled nation. He has, it is true, rejected many of the romantic excesses of chivalry, but at heart he remains a footloose adventurer, who "desires no more fame than his good lance and sword may acquire him." We cannot help but like his high spirits ("he was gay, good-humored, and fond of manhood in every rank of life"). His heroics are extraordinary by any standard, and timely beyond belief. Perhaps most admirable of all is his unselfish and humane desire to end discrimination between Normans and Saxons and to forge an English nation out of their brotherhood. But for all that he may have learned by watching Robin Hood administer the affairs of his forest kingdom, Richard is a poor king. And to the end of his brief reign he will remain a man to whom "the personal glory which he acquired by his own deeds of arms, was far more dear to his excited imagination than that which a course of policy and wisdom would have spread around his government."

Prince John

Richard's younger brother, who will ascend the throne within six year after this book ends, is as unlike him as a man can be. He is an unscrupulous and crafty politician who might have been a successful conspirator but for his uncontrollable temper. Nearly every word he speaks conceals some political design, and he is hypocritical by nature. He is a dandy, vain an ultra-refined. His clothes are gorgeous and his manners correct. But he has none of the chivalric virtues that raise his brother above the common cut, nor any of the human sympathy and tact that might have made him a satisfactory king.

Waldemar Fitzurse

Prince John's right-hand man. The genius behind John's conspiracy is a shrewd, calculating, yet sensitive man. He swallows his master's insults and abuse in the hope of great reward when he makes John king. His advice is nearly always sound and his political manipulations are masterful. Only when he steps out of character-when he becomes the soldier instead of the counselor-does he fail. When De Bracy hurries from Torquilstone to warn the Prince that Richard has returned, John inveigles Waldemar into leading an ambush on the king. Once away from his element, the intrigues of court life, Fitzurse botches the assassination attempt. He is taken prisoner and with him is lost the mind and impetus of the rebellion.

Reginald Front-De-Boeuf

One of the powerful barons supporting John's plot, a neighbor of Cedric of Rotherwood. Like Ulrica, he is a Gothic stereotype, a monster of a man physically and morally. Scott describes him as a giant several times, and we eventually discover that his vices are at least as enormous. Wamba mentions him first as a legendary Norman baron, whose very name strikes terror into the hearts of disgruntled Saxons. His name crops up in the conversation of several major characters before his appearance at Ashby. He loses to the Disinherited Knight in the lists there and, perhaps in retaliation, leagues ith De Bracy to snatch Rowena. Fitzurse warns De Bracy that "he is a falcon well accustomed to pounce on a partridge, and to hold his prey fast," but his interest is easily diverted to the wealthy Isaac, who has unexpectedly fallen into the catch. In the most distasteful of the three dialogues in the castle, Front-de-Boeuf threatens and tortures the ancient Jew with methodical zest. But it is only when Ulrica reveals the sordid story of her humiliation and revenge at Torquilstone that the worst of De Bracy's crimes comes to light. At her instigation, he has slain his own father after a drunken brawl. She knows him as a demon whose evil is too base for human ears, and she makes it her business to embitter his dying moments by raking up the memory of his crimes and leaving him to be burned alive in the castle he usurped. Scott seems to have conceived Front-de-Boeuf at first only as a dreadful name, and then a useful confederate for Bois-Guilbert and De Bracy. But, although he continues to have little direct effect upon the plot of the novel, the sinister possibilities of his character develop once the action moves to his castle. The unspeakable blackness of his soul and the terrible agony of his death are in the true spirit of Gothic sensationalism.

Lucas Beaumanoir

Grand Master of the Order of Knights Templar. A conscientious priest who finds the antidote to the worldliness and blasphemies of his brothers in fanaticism. He sees witches and hobgoblins everywhere tempting the weak souls of believers, and he regards it as is solemn responsibility to rid the world of them. His resulting prejudice against nonconformists and strangers nearly costs the saintly Rebecca her life. Nevertheless there is more of human compassion and genuine virtue in a man who honestly believes in his religion than in base hypocrites like Aymer and Bois-Guilbert. Scott may have this in mind in rewarding the Grand Master with a courageous and respectable exit speech.

Maurice De Bracy

A misguided, irresponsible nobleman whose passion for Rowena has gotten the best of his reason. Although a Norman and leader of the Free Company (a band of soldiers-for-hire), he is indifferent to Prince John's political designs and belatedly returns to love and respect for Richard. Despite the infamous abduction he carries out, he is clearly the least villainous of the black threesome he leads. His treatment of Rowena is forward, but at all times respectful and polite. He keeps Ivanhoe's presence in the castle a secret from Front-de-Boeuf-a vaguely charitable act. His conduct during the siege is as valiant, if not so furious, as his comrades'. After a brave struggle with Richard he resigns honorably and keeps the terms of his surrender to the letter. Disregarding Prince John's attractive bait (the promise of high office) he leaves the country as Richard had commanded, regretful that his part in the conspiracy has deprived him of his sovereign's trust. Besides being a late-repentant demi-villain, De Bracy represents the courtly lover at his worst. His gestures and words are by the book, but in the context Scott provides for him he seems foolish and adolescent. His sacrifice of political obligations to the idol of his passions may conform to the principles of courtly love, but it will hardly do for a true Englishman. None of the characters of whom Scott approves most highly-Ivanhoe, Richard, Locksley-would think of putting love for a woman before duties to his family, his nation, and his personal honor.

Albert Malvoisin

Preceptor of Templestowe and brother of Philip, a powerful Norman baron. Somewhat like a modern fight manager, Malvoisin grooms and conditions a younger Templar with bright prospects (Bois-Guilbert) for the role of Grand Master of the Order. He is, like Fitzurse, explicitly a kingmaker, hoping to ride to glory on the coattails of another man's career. But their differences are instructive. Malvoisin is not a politician but a priest; he is his protégé's superior rather than his servant. He is, moreover, the most accomplished liar in the novel. Other characters may be misguided or self-interested or even hypocritical, but none depends so extensively upon the lie to gain his ends. In the comparison with Fitzurse, therefore, Malvoisin is far more contemptible and deserves the traitor's death Richard metes out to him.

Brian De Bois-Guilbert (The Templar)

Bois-Guilbert is the main antagonist in the novel. He is a Knight Templar and ex-Crusader who aspires to become Grand Master of his Order as the first stepping stone in a scheme of world conquest. He is totally amoral and an atheist despite his priestly vows. Disappointed love for a woman drove him to join the Order and it is clear from his first appearance onward that his holy calling has not dimmed his passions. At Cedric's hall he sets his sights on Rowena, only to change his mind on Seeing Rebecca's unveiled face at Ashby. He badgers Rebecca tirelessly, at both Torquilstone and Templestowe, until his passions get the better of him on the day of her trial-by-combat. Despite moments of insight into his character, the Templar is never a sympathetic figure. But he is better drawn than either of his two co-villains; and his particular brand of villainy is neither so empty-headed as De Bracy's nor so unnatural as Front-de-Boeuf's.

Prior Aymer Of Jorvaulx

Norman priest (a Cistercian monk) and one of Prince John's party at Ashby. As the brother of a powerful Norman baron, it was quite natural in these times for him to have become a priest since so few options were available to noblemen without fortunes. (The law of primogeniture provided that only a firstborn son could inherit his father's wealth.) His rich robes, jewels, and talk of women suggest that he has not yet accomplished the divorce from worldly things that the church expected of its servants. He detests violence, however, and has made a study of ingratiating himself with all kinds of men to avoid it. Unlike Friar Tuck, who doffs his religion whenever the occasion demands, Aymer uses his holy office to his personal advantage. He is cowardly, bigoted, and wholly derelict in his spiritual duties. If Friar Tuck is a distant relative of an English country parson, Aymer anticipates the degeneration of the Catholic priesthood during the Renaissance which brought on the Reformation.

JEWS

Isaac Of York

A Jewish merchant and moneylender, reluctant treasurer of John's conspiracy. Isaac is a Jewish stereotype, ridiculously preoccupied with hoarding his fortune. Scott's attitude toward him seems curiously mixed. Isaac's stinginess appears to be justified by the hardships and oppressions his race must suffer in "Christian" Europe; yet Scott seems to enjoy caricaturing him Isaac has his moment of glory in the scene with Front-de-Boeuf, but on the whole he serves as comic relief and an ironical contrast to Rebecca's charity and benevolence.

Rebecca

Of the thousands of characters Scott created none lingers in the mind like Rebecca. She does not appear until Chapter Seven, or speak until Chapter Ten. She seems to have very little to do with the main plot of the novel. Yet her fascination remains long after we have forgotten all else about Ivanhoe, just as it remains with Ivanhoe long after she has fled to Spain. Her combination of dark Oriental beauty and steadfast purity beguiles us. She is the perfect woman, the dream love just beyond the reach of men in society. (Remember that she first and last appears to Ivanhoe in a dream.)

One aspect of her desirability is that Rebecca is an exciting and voluptuous woman. Scott draws her portrait with unmistakable overtones of sensuality. The description in Chapter Seven includes a lingering survey of her "lovely neck and bosom," made even more appealing by "the three uppermost [clasps of her vest] . . . left unfastened on account of the heat, which something enlarged the prospect to which we allude." She is capable of deep, smoldering passion, as in her undeclared and unwilling love for Ivanhoe. When she exposes herself to the public at Ashby to make room for the wounded Ivanhoe in her litter, the effect is the same as if she had disrobed. For it is here that the Templar first fixes his penetrating gaze upon her and conceives the tremendous passion that is to be his undoing. The act of removing her veil before the throng at Templestowe is even more explicitly sexual: "it suits not a maiden to be disrobed by such rude grooms," she says as she bares her face "in which bashfulness contended with dignity." No one is more excited by this sight than "the younger knights [who] told each other with their eyes, in silent correspondence, that Brian's best apology was in the power of her real charms. . . ." Indeed, this kind of hidden thrill looks suspiciously like the "dirty little secret" D. H. Lawrence was to deplore in our time-a kind of compensation and substitute for the real thing. But this is not to deny that it constitutes an important part of Rebecca's effect on us.

At the same time Rebecca's moral superiority (in no way inconsistent with her beauty) is established every time she confronts another character. Isaac hardly seems fit to be her father. Ivanhoe is certainly no match for her; in fact we marvel that such a splendid woman could come to love so shallow a man. Bois-Guilbert has more of her spirit and pride, but her virtue overcomes his villainy without much of a struggle. The most telling contrast is with Rowena, who is a pale, limp lily beside Rebecca's lush, brilliant Rose of Sharon.

IVANHOE

ESSAY QUESTIONS AND ANSWERS

Question: What is the **theme** of *Ivanhoe?*

Answer: It is difficult to find a consistent **theme** in any of Scott's novels, but there seem to be two interconnected **themes** at the core of *Ivanhoe:* the evils of bigotry, and the compromise between heroic ideals and present reality. The book begins simply enough with an undeclared civil war in England between good Saxons and their sinister Norman conquerors. Our sympathy is with Cedric and his countrymen because they have been the victims of oppression and discrimination. But when Isaac the Jew appears against this background, the convenient moral distinction between the races breaks down. Isaac replaces the Saxons as underdog in the book, thus removing the sentimental haze that has blurred our judgment. In the next few chapters Isaac elicits the bigotry of nearly every character in the book, from the Saxon jester to the Norman Prince. The Saxon has not rejected bigotry simply because he has been its victim. If Saxons can mistreat a wretched Jew with less justification than the Normans have for oppressing them, perhaps our approval of the Saxon cause has been too hasty. Perhaps they are as much to blame for their present difficulties as the Norman intruders.

Cedric's behavior is cast in a new light: disinheritance of his son, advocacy of the unworthy Athelstane, blind preference for all things Saxon, inflexible racist vows, etc. In all these things Cedric has acted from bigotry rather than good sense. Here and throughout the remainder of the book Scott depicts a world sick with irrational racial and religious hatred. And it is this moral sickness, rather than political and cultural differences, that divides England and keeps it weak. The return of Ivanhoe and King Richard is a victory for England and for tolerance. Ivanhoe is living proof of the wisdom of merging the two races. Using Ivanhoe's example, Richard has begun to erase the artificial barriers between Norman and Saxon and to restore a kind of impartial enlightened government to the throne. Scott remains cynical at the book's end for he knows that the war against bigotry is yet to be won. Rebecca and Isaac must, therefore, find a safer home than England, as a reminder that bigotry dies hard.

Bigotry is only one consequence of a broader human dilemma that Scott often writes about. Before men can live at peace with themselves and their society they must put away the dreams and ideals of the past and accept life as they find it. Cedric's love of a past that can never be recaptured is the cause of his bigotry. But it also makes him a misfit, an **anachronism**, in everything he does. What seemed a noble cause-Saxon restoration-has become ridiculous in the face of social change and progress. When the inevitable end of Cedric's dream comes he cannot accept and enjoy what remains of life. De Bracy's chivalric tomfoolery is another illusion that has outlived its usefulness; and Richard's knight-errantry, Scott tells us, is the fatal weakness of even that great man. Beaumanoir, on the religious side, carries with him into exile the bright hopes of a pious order of priests in a God-fearing world. In some important way, none of these men has successfully bridged the gap between past and present or accepted the modern definitions of real and ideal. They all prefer chasing will-o'-the-wisps to knuckling down to hard fact and the business of facing life on its own terms. In fact it is impossible to point to any major character in the novel who has met this test with distinction and Scott's approval. This **theme**, which David Daiches believes binds the Scottish novels together, did not cease to interest Scott when he changed the setting of his stories. In any case it is clear that Scott's aim in *Ivanhoe* was not to glorify the past, but to hold it up as a mirror to modern society.

Question: Discuss Scott's attitude toward Chivalry.

Answer: There are three kinds of chivalric characters in the novel: the knight-errant, the courtly lover, and a warrior-lover somewhere between the two. The knight-errant, typified by Richard, is a fearless soldier-of-fortune who takes his excitement and honor where he finds them. Richard's detour in the forest to help Locksley liberate Torquilstone is a perfect example of the kind of exploit such knights made it their mission to perform. Any worthy person in distress might invoke the service of a knight-errant. In a world bounded only by the influence of the Christian church, such deeds were all that a man could wish to accomplish. But as the Middle Ages drew to a close nations began to emerge within the boundaries of Christendom. A man's duty was increasingly commanded by the land of his birth rather than by Rome. Individual acts of heroism became less possible and less meaningful in a world of nation states. Knight-errantry thus became an indulgence instead of a service-especially if the knight held a position of responsibility in his nation. In that case he owed his life not to God, honor, or the few poor wretches he might save by his deeds; but to the past, present, and future of his country. Richard's attempt to perpetuate chivalry beyond its natural life span had become an irresponsible breach of solemn obligations. It is a black mark against Richard that he remembers his knightly vows before those of his coronation.

The second aspect of chivalry, courtly love, fares even worse in this novel. De Bracy's childish imagination inspires him with the idea of sweeping Rowena off her feet with his dash and courtesy. He seems to be playing an innocent game as he disguises himself for the abduction and anticipates the bliss of Rowena's love. The illusion quickly fades during his interview with her at Torquilstone. His flowery speeches and extravagant **metaphors** are wilted by the real despair and pain that Rowena suffers. There was a time when a woman as beautiful and well-born as Rowena would have known this was all love-play, a **convention**, a mere proof of love. But in a world that has rejected such empty rituals nothing could be more absurd. The man who could waste his youth and energy languishing for the love of a tease had become an object of ridicule (or fear, if he had power). Such love has never completely died away. In Scott's time it found a new birth in the love lyrics of the Romantic poets. But it is clear that this was one more extreme that the conservative Scott could not tolerate.

In *Ivanhoe* we find a compromise with chivalry toward which an honorable and responsible modern man might strive. Ivanhoe is a brave and skillful warrior, but he never neglects his duties. Every time he raises his lance Ivanhoe is discharging some debt or obligation that any reasonable man would honor. His itch to fight at Torquilstone may be explained by his illness and be offset by his attempt to play the conscience of the king somewhat later. As a lover he rises well above his competition (Athelstane), but short of De Bracy's lunacy. For his time and his culture, Ivanhoe has made an adequate and satisfactory adjustment to modern life. But for Scott and his readers he is nearly as foolish as De Bracy. His dispute with Rebecca over the glories of warfare reminds us that, for all his virtues, Ivanhoe has a long way to go. His defense of bloodshed in the name of chivalry is nothing short of barbarous to the modern ear. Even in this sugar-coated form, therefore, chivalry is a prime target for Scott's irony.

Question: What is meant by Scott's "sense of the past"?

Answer: Scott approaches the problem of writing about the past with the conventional assumption that human nature does not change with the passage of time. Men, the theory goes, are basically the same today as they have always been. This premise allows the novelist to construct historical characters with the same passions and responses as modern ones-men and women who think, feel, and behave much as we do. After all, people fear death, love their children, worship God, and strive for wealth and glory, whether they were born thirty years ago or three thousand. But there is nothing new in this. Nearly every learned man before Scott who had written about the past began at this same point: they all agreed that the past was very much like the present. Scott's innovation was to assume this, and to stress rather the differences between past and present - the details that had nothing to do with eternal human nature, but existed rather on the surface of life. Styles of dress and architecture, politics and commerce; religious ritual and social customs - this is the mine that Scott worked for over thirty novels. He studied the fashions and manners of a past era until he had reconstructed it in his mind. Language was probably the most important study of all. Since the language spoken during Richard's reign, for example, was undecipherable to modern readers, there could be no thought of complete authenticity in the dialogue. But if a writer were careful to omit all exclusively modern **allusions** and expressions, and to spice his sentences with archaic words and constructions, he might achieve the effect of authenticity - that is, his readers would think they were listening in on an ancient conversation. Similar modifications and compromises were made with other aspects of medieval life. (Scott says, for example, that the tortures and atrocities he describes are mild beside the real thing.) But the result was, as he had hoped, a magnificent evocation of the past. Never had readers felt so strongly the atmosphere and texture of a bygone era; never had it seemed quite so real before. The colors, the sounds, the broad panorama, and the minute details-it was all there on the page before them. The more vivid and immediate Scott's portrait, however, the greater the distance readers felt between their own and that far-off time. By giving the past shape and size, Scott helped to fix it in time, as well. And by fusing the novel of manners with the popular romance, Scott created a new kind of literature: the historical novel.

Question: What is the function of the Jewish characters in *Ivanhoe?*

Answer: Rebecca and Isaac appear to have very little to do either with the political or the personal affairs of the novel. His role as John's financier is never fully developed; in fact it seems merely an excuse for putting Jews in the same place at the same time as other important characters. Rebecca concealed her love for Ivanhoe well enough not to let him know it, and therefore even her direct effect upon the plot is limited to the Templestowe episode. In short, Scott seems to have deliberately made a place for them at the center of his book despite their incidental importance to the plot. A number of explanations are possible. The simplest is that a friend suggested the idea of using Jewish characters to Scott. Perhaps he liked the novelty of the idea. Scott, according to Rosenberg, "was the first to give the Jews any kind of popular prominence in the English novel." Perhaps the story of Rebecca Gratz moved him to commemorate her in one of his characters. But when we consider the major **theme** of the novel and Isaac's relation to it, a more likely answer emerges. Isaac and Rebecca are in the book to suffer.

Normans and Saxons may hate each other, but everyone hates the Jew. Even Ivanhoe does not hide his contempt for Isaac, although he has just saved the old man's life. Nor does he leave any doubt in Rebecca's mind about their prospects for romance once she tells him who she is. If the hero of the book is capable of such intolerance, we should not be appalled at the brutality of Front-de-Boeuf or the Templar's frank sexuality. But do they serve merely to demonstrate that all men, from the best to the worst, are capable of blind prejudice? Edgar Rosenberg thinks not: [they are] "a kind of critical norm, the yardstick by which Scott can measure the abnormities and abnormalities of their oppressors." Moreover they are "exponents of that critical, basically anti-sentimental attitude toward chivalry which gives the novel its essential content." Isaac pays his debt to Ivanhoe but worries incessantly about the suit of armor. When Rebecca is taken to Templestowe he raises no siege, but goes himself to pay a cash ransom in exchange for her. Only the interference of a wild-eyed idealist (Beaumanoir) prevents him from making a deal. Rebecca, unlike the Christian ladies in the book, learns the useful art of healing and practices it with skill and tenderness. Predictably, she argues with Ivanhoe when he praises warfare and senseless slaughter. Yet for all her pacifism she protects her honor with her life (Rowena's defenses, by contrast, seem exhausted once she has a good cry-fortunately her kidnapper is less aggressive than Rebecca's!) Taken all in all, these are the practical actions of a resourceful people who will endure; who had scrapped worn-out ideals and meet the challenge of survival. But they do more than survive: they prevail. "For the first time in English literature, the Jews alone are right and everybody else is wrong. The outcast defines the community; the scapegoat indicts the king." Their emigration to Spain at the close of the novel is, therefore, more than a convenient way of disposing of Rowena's rival. It is a commentary on the moral condition of England. When two Godfearing, innocent people like these cannot live in peace and safety in this country, neither a glittering wedding ceremony nor a gallant, well-meaning king can cover up the underlying fault that makes it possible. The joyous note on which the novel ends is thin and hollow, and certain to die quickly away. The Jewish characters are more than a bonus, a stroke of luck, or an interesting novelty: they are indispensable to the thematic development of the novel.

QUESTIONS FOR DISCUSSION

1. Why is Ivanhoe returning alone from the Crusades?
2. Why has Cedric disowned his son?
3. Who won the wager between Bois-Guilbert and Aymer?
4. Give examples of the importance of languages in this book.
5. Does Scott favor either side in the conflict between Normans and Saxons?
6. Why does the Templar help De Bracy in his plot to abduct Rowena?
7. What use does Scott make of bugles in his story?
8. What is Ulrica's function in the novel?
9. To what extent does Scott employ comic relief or comic subplots? What purpose do they serve?

10. Why does Rebecca love Ivanhoe? Why does she wish she didn't?

11. What are Ivanhoe's feelings for Rebecca?

12. Why does Cedric forgive his son?

13. Why does Scott contrive to bring Athelstane back to life?

14. What is the significance of the Templar's manner of death? Has Scott prepared us for it?

15. Why does Rebecca slip away from Templestowe before thanking Ivanhoe for saving her?

16. Why do Rebecca and Isaac leave for Spain at the end of the book?

17. Discuss the relation between the chapter-tags (epigraphs) and the chapters they head.

18. Discuss the animal **imagery** in Ivanhoe.

19. What is Scott's final judgment of Beaumanoir?

20. To what extent is Ivanhoe useful as an introduction to feudalism? How well does it compare with what you know of the subject?

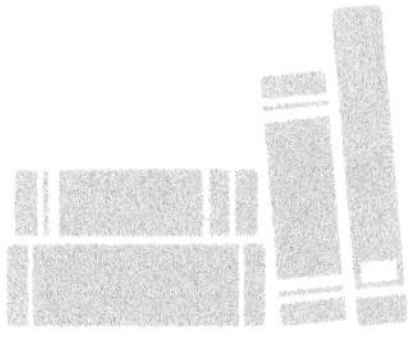

THE HEART OF MIDLOTHIAN

In the year 1737 Scotland was between two wars: the ill-fated rebellions of 1715 and 1745 that brought that proud nation once and for all under British rule. The spirit that had launched the '15 and soon would explode into the '45 was not at rest during peacetime. The traces of British oppression were everywhere to remind Scotsmen of their bondage. Many daring young men defied the government by smuggling goods across the Scottish border, since they considered English import duties "an unjust aggression upon their ancient liberties." Two of the bravest of these had been caught in the act, imprisoned in the Tollbooth prison (nicknamed the Heart of Midlothian) in Edinburgh, and sentenced to die for their crime. The younger, Geordie Robertson, made a successful escape on the way to the gallows, but Andrew Wilson went to his death as prescribed by the harsh laws of that time. The captain of the execution detail, Porteous by name, had made Wilson's last moments so unpleasant, however, that the Scottish mob that came to watch the hanging now clamored for revenge against him in the dead man's name. Panic-stricken, Porteous ordered his soldiers to fire on the crowd, and seven persons died in the barrage that followed. For his hasty act Porteous was himself condemned to hang. But on the day assigned for his execution, with an enormous crowd waiting to witness his death, a last-minute reprieve from Queen Caroline of England postponed the event for six weeks. Later that night an angry mob, led by the outlaw Robertson, forced its way into the Tollbooth and lynched Porteous. Only one of the mob, the young Reverend Reuben Butler, said a word on his behalf. Butler had been to the Tollbooth earlier in the day to inquire after a young serving-girl imprisoned for child murder. The girl, Effie Deans, had worked for some friends of his (Bartoline and Mrs. Saddletree) in their saddle shop, and this charitable couple asked Butler to see what he could do for her. When the jailer refused to let him visit Effie, Butler made his way toward his home outside Edinburgh. It was at the gate of the city that the lynch mob intercepted him and, recognizing him as a clergyman, forced him to return to the Tollbooth with them. When the gates of the prison were locked on the rioters they burned them down. All but three of the prisoners inside were freed. One, Porteous, was dragged out of concealment to answer for his sins. The second was a thief named Ratcliffe who claimed to have gone straight. And the last was Effie Deans, who ignored Robertson's passionate insistence that she escape. Outside, Butler's speech had failed to sway the mob from its murderous course, so he did what he could to prepare the unlucky Porteous for the life hereafter. The hanging followed immediately and before long the bewildered minister was on his way home again.

Butler's concern for Effie went much deeper than he had let on to the Saddletrees. Her father, Douce David Deans, owned the tenant farm nearest his own when he was a child, and paid for his religious education when his grandmother (who reared him) could not afford it. Her older half-sister, Jeanie Deans, had been his childhood sweetheart, and only his difficulty in finding a vicarage delayed their marriage. He remembered Effie as a lovely and vivacious girl, who loved to dance and sing despite the strict upbringing her Presbyterian father imposed upon both his daughters. Her free spirits had often been a source of irritation to her father, and when Mrs. Saddletree (a distant relative) invited Effie to take a position with her in Edinburgh everyone rejoiced at the idea. But shortly after her arrival in the city Effie fell into a physical and emotional depression. She returned home after some months with the Saddletrees, and her sister Jeanie needed no hints to discover the cause of her sister's condition: Effie had had a baby. But she would say nothing of the child or its father. Unable to account for the whereabouts and health of her infant, she was arrested for the crime of child-murder and returned to Edinburgh and the Tollbooth prison. Her father collapsed at the shock of this disclosure. He had always been a man of God, who lived by high principles and rigid moral convictions. Effie's sin, therefore, plunged him into despair and he refused to lift a finger to help her evade the just punishment for her pleasures and evildoing. As Butler proceeded toward his home at St. Leonard's he met a dark, handsome, and vaguely familiar young man. Without identifying himself, he asked the good Reverend to carry a message to Jeanie Deans. She was to meet him alone at moonrise that evening at a certain deserted spot known as Muschat's Cairn. When the young man had gone Butler was uncertain whether to be afraid or jealous: afraid that "the fiery eye, the abrupt demeanor ... the features, handsome, but now clouded with pride, now disturbed with suspicion, now inflamed with passion," were those of an evil demon; jealous at the thought that he might be Jeanie's secret "earthly lover," judging from the "summary and unceremonious authority" he had assumed over her affairs. When he arrived at the Dean's cottage at St. Leonard's Crags, Butler paid his respects to Effie's grieving father. The arrival of Mr. Saddletree soon after gave Butler a chance to talk with Jeanie. He delivered the young stranger's message, but threatened to break off their engagement when she could not explain who he was. Meanwhile Saddletree and Deans were having a heated argument about helping Effie.

In an effort to persuade the old man to act on Effie's behalf, Saddletree painted her predicament for them all to see. She had confessed to bearing an illegitimate child and, by Scottish law, if she could neither produce the infant nor prove that she had disclosed her pregnancy to another (thus proving her intention to have the child in good faith), she would surely be found guilty of child-murder and sentenced to die. The best hope seemed to be to bribe some influential magistrates and government officers (the Laird of Dumbiedikes, Dean's landlord and a hapless suitor for Jeanie's hand, offered thirty pounds to cover the expense). But Saddletree let drop that Effie had spoken of a woman who cared for her during the delivery of her child. In the hope of finding this woman out, Butler returned again to the Tollbooth prison to speak with Effie.

No sooner was he admitted to the prison than he found himself being interrogated about the riot the night before. He himself had been seen at the head of the mob and was considered a prime suspect. He told all he knew about the riot, satisfying the officers of the court that he had committed no crime, but they seemed more interested in his encounter with the stranger on the road home. Back at St. Leonard's that evening, Jeanie went to keep her rendezvous with the same young man. Her mind was full of the superstitions of the region and as she made her way toward the appointed place she was terrified at the mystery that awaited her. At first the stranger tried to take advantage of her fears as a means of bending her to his will. He was the father of Effie's child, he said, and knew her to be innocent of the charge laid against her: "She is guiltless-guiltless of everything but of having trusted a villain." The law that would convict her, he went on, had but one loophole: it was in Jeanie's power to save her sister with a single word. She had only to swear that Effie had told her she was pregnant. But Jeanie remembered clearly that her sister had never mentioned this dreadful fact; and she could not lie before "the God, whose name I must call on to witness the truth of what I say." The stranger argued desperately that God would overlook the deed in favor of the motive for good that prompted it. But there was no shaking her refusal to lie: "I may not do evil, even that good may come out of it." Their conversation came to an abrupt end when the stranger heard a distant but familiar voice singing a song of warning. Madge Wildfire, a demented amazon of a woman and his one-time sweetheart, had been forced to lead a party of constables to Muschat's Cairn. For it was learned that the man Butler had spoken to the morning after the Porteous lynching was none other than the condemned fugitive, Geordie Robertson. Moreover, with the help of the testimony from Butler and Ratcliffe (the reformed thief), the authorities linked Robertson to both Effie Deans and the riots. But the elusive young blackguard escaped the trap that had been laid for him when he heard Madge's song.

Somewhat later a letter signed by "one of [the] slayers" of Porteous crossed the desk of Mr. Bailie Middleburgh, a magistrate. It stated that Effie was innocent and that her sister, Jeanie, held the key to her salvation. Middleburgh visited St. Leonard's in the hope of finding evidence to support the allegations of the letter. Evidence there was none, but he did persuade David Deans to release his daughter Jeanie from any religious scruples about appearing in court in order to give testimony for her sister. When Deans tried to convey his wish to Jeanie she misunderstood him to be asking her to lie for Effie. The pressure on Jeanie became even greater on the evening before Effie's trial when she visited her sister in the Tollbooth. Effie, humble and resigned to her death at first, changed her tone once the name of Robertson entered the conversation. The thought that her lover had risked his life to rescue her gave Effie a new will to live. She cursed Jeanie's inflexible moral code if it would cost an innocent woman her life. Robertson would not have hesitated to lie for her. For

Jeanie, however, lying would be worse than dying: "Oh, if it stude wi' me to save ye wi' the risk of my life!" When the time came for them to part Effie relented and embraced her sister. She agreed to accept whatever decision Jeanie made; but she could offer nothing else in the way of evidence to clear herself. Jeanie left the cell even more troubled than when she had entered.

Effie's trial was a long but clear-cut affair. Her case rested almost entirely on the hope that her sister would swear that she had known of the pregnancy from Effie's own lips. When Jeanie entered the courtroom, "Effie, with the whole expression of her countenance altered, from that of confused shame and dismay, to an eager, imploring, almost ecstatic earnestness of entreaty, with outstretched hands, hair streaming back, eyes raised eagerly to her sister's face, and glistening through tears, exclaimed, in a tone which went through the heart of all who heard her-'O Jeanie, Jeanie, save me, save me!' "The oath of honor was given and Jeanie began to answer the questions of Mr. Fairbrother, Effie's attorney. Gradually he came around to the subject of Effie's visit to St. Leonard's during her employment with Mrs. Saddletree. Did you ask her about her condition? "I asked her what ailed her." And her answer? "Nothing . . . Alack! Alack! she never breathed a word to me about it." Davie Deans collapsed in the courtroom at this final confirmation of Effie's guilt. The jury had no need to deliberate at length. Despite the nearly unanimous belief that the law was a cruel one, according to its letter Effie was pronounced guilty. She was sentenced to be hanged until dead.

It was Mr. Saddletree who delivered this dreadful verdict to Jeanie-only the king could save Effie now, she said. Instead of wilting in despair, Jeanie asked eagerly: "But can the king give her mercy?" Mrs. Saddletree reminded her that Porteous had been reprieved by the Queen. Yes, it could be done. Suddenly

Jeanie put aside her sorrow and turned to the task before her. The providence in which she placed her faith had not failed her. She asked her father's blessing on her "errand" and hurried to the Tollbooth to tell Effie of her plan. "I will go to London and beg [a] pardon from the king and queen." Ratcliffe, the reformed thief, had been made the turnkey of the Tollbooth for his part in the near-capture of Robertson. He advised Jeanie not to go directly to the king, but to see the Duke of Argyle first, for he was a friend of Scotland and a favorite with the queen. He also described a safe-conduct for her in case she met with highwaymen along the road. Lack of money was the first great obstacle in her adventure. She appealed to the Laird of Dumbiedikes, who had long hoped to make her his wife, but refused to bargain her love for his money. Only when she turned to leave did the foolish Laird think better of his niggardly behavior and press the money on her. Next she told Reuben Butler of her intention. When he could not dissuade her, he offered to marry her so that he could protect her on the way to London. But again she showed her mettle by refusing marriage on such grounds.

The distance from Edinburgh to London was nearly four hundred miles, a perilous enough journey on horseback in those days. Jeanie set forth alone to walk the entire distance. She met many good people on the road but eventually fell into the hands of a vicious pair of highwaymen. She produced Ratcliffe's safe-conduct, which seemed to alter their plan to "strip the wrench, and send her begging back to her own beggarly country." The thieves took her instead to a hut in the woods where they turned her over to two gypsy women: the crazed Madge Wildfire, and her wicked mother, who was known as "Mother Blood." Jeanie learned that Mother Blood had hired the thieves to terrorize her and to frustrate the mission she had undertaken. Years before Madge Wildfire (then bearing the respectable name of Murdockson) had borne Robertson a child. Rather than allow this unhappy incident to interfere with her plan to marry Madge to a rich old gentleman, her mother slew the child. Not only did this foul murder ruin Madge's betrothal, it took her sanity as well. Ever since then she and her mother had been outlaws, although the thought had never left Mother Blood's mind that Robertson would someday marry Madge. If Effie were released from prison Robertson would almost certainly marry her, and this was an eventuality that Mother Blood had no intention of permitting. It was for this reason that Jeanie now found herself a prisoner and her expedition to London interrupted.

The next morning Madge invited Jeanie to take a walk with her. Sensing an opportunity for escape, Jeanie accepted. Along the way Madge began to lament about her own dead child and asked if Jeanie had ever had a baby. "Jeanie replied in the negative. 'Ay; but your sister had, though - and I ken what came o't too!" This dark hint set Jeanie's curiosity burning, but the more she pressed the maniac the less she could get out of her. In time they came upon a pleasant English village where Madge, acting out an **episode** from *Pilgrim's Progress*, planned to find the house of "the Interpreter," one Mr. Staunton. Together the disheveled girls entered the local church where Madge seemed to be well-known. When the service was over Jeanie, hoping for sanctuary in this place, refused to return to the gypsy camp with Madge. The cruel taunts of the townspeople drove the madwoman away in time to spare Jeanie a fight for her freedom. She next sought out the house of the minister, Mr. Staunton, but he had only begun to hear her story when the groans of his ailing son called him away. After a long wait Jeanie was again shown into the "master's" presence. This time, instead of the minister, she stood before his son, George Staunton. To her amazement he was the same Geordie Robertson who had dishonored her sister - the mysterious stranger from Muschat's Cairn. He completed the story Jeanie had heard only in part at the outlaw's hideout.

He was the son of a wealthy minister and had, in his wild youth, sported with the "giddy" daughter of one of his father's servants, Meg Murdockson. Meg had "endeavored to promote [Madge's] marriage with an old and wealthy churl in the neighborhood." His father discovered the affair and sent his son abroad; and by the time George returned Meg and Madge had left the village in disgrace. He became "engaged in desperate adventures" under the guidance of Andrew Wilson. It was also at about this time that he met Effie, who frequently sneaked out at night to meet him. When she became pregnant he appealed to his father for the means to make an honest woman of her. But to his dismay his father disowned him instead. Desperate, he took up the work that nearly brought him to the gallows. He did the best he could for Effie while he lay in prison, with the intention of marrying her as soon as he could escape. He had renewed his acquaintance with Meg and Madge Murdockson in Edinburgh and, believing them to bear him no grudge, paid them to care for Effie during her confinement. By the time he had escaped and revenged himself on Porteous, Effie was in jail. Meg Murdockson professed to know nothing of what had become of Effie or the son she bore since the night she left a sick bed to run away. When every other means of saving Effie had failed-raiding the Tollbooth, telling Jeanie to lie at the trial, etc. - Staunton was on his way to London to give himself up as a wanted criminal in return for Effie's freedom. Before he had gone ten miles his horse collapsed and injured him severely. At this point the Reverend Staunton entered the room and ended their conversation. He provided the girl with a night's lodgings and transportation to the nearest coach-route to London. George Staunton completed his remarks to Jeanie in a letter, in which he begged her not to hesitate to trade his life for Effie's if she could not obtain mercy.

Not long afterward the Duke of Argyll received an unusual caller in the library of his London home. A lone Scottish lass asked him to intercede with the king on behalf of her unjustly condemned sister. He was more curious than expectant when he had her admitted, but as Jeanie poured out the story of Effie's trial and her own hard journey to save her he could not help being touched. He had long been a friend of Scotland and this particular girl impressed him so favorably with her honestly and courage that, despite the uncertainty of Scottish politics, he promised to do everything in his power to aid her sister. Jeanie stayed with Mrs. Glass, a cousin, who owned a small tobacco shop in town, while two days passed without a word from the Duke. But on the third day Mr. Archibald, the Duke's gentleman, called upon Jeanie and drove her to meet his master. The Duke's news was good, for he had "asked an audience of a lady whose interest with the king is very high." While the carriage rolled toward their appointment, he advised Jeanie to tell her story "as plainly and boldly" as she had in his library. They arrived at a lovely country estate and, as the Duke expected, the lady received Jeanie's story warmly and sympathetically. Only after the lady promised to speak to the king and presented her with a memento of the occasion did Jeanie discover that she had been speaking to Queen Caroline herself. The pardon was certain to be granted now, although one condition was eventually attached to it: Effie would have to remain in exile for a period of fourteen years. On the way back to Mrs. Glass's shop the Duke made plans for speeding Jeanie and her glad tidings back to Edinburgh. He parted with her only after she had promised to send him a home-made Scottish cheese. Jeanie's visit to London had lasted three weeks in all, and on the morning of her departure the Duke and his family all turned out to bid her farewell.

Somewhat later her carriage drew near the ancient city of Carlisle. Jeanie caught sight of Madge Wildfire being persecuted by a mob that had just hanged her mother, Meg Murdockson. She did what she could to save the poor wretch, but Madge died with the words of an old **ballad** on her lips. Jeanie now despaired of ever finding out the truth about Effie's infant son. On the ride home Jeanie observed that the carriage did not take the accustomed road to Glasgow; soon she found herself on the lovely island of Roseneath in the Firth of Clyde. And there, waiting on the shore, was her father, David Deans. Their reunion was dampened by the news that Effie had eloped with Staunton (or Robertson) within three days after her release from prison. And Jeanie's thoughts were already heavy with the thought that she had not heard one word from Reuben Butler during her absence. But there was good news, too. As they walked toward the nearby lodge, Deans explained that he had been invited to superintend the Duke of Argyle's magnificent experimental farm in Dumbartonshire. The hard life at St. Leonard's Crags was behind them. An even greater surprise awaited her inside the lodge, however, when her father introduced the local parson (a new man): "She had indeed seen him before, for it was no other than Reuben Butler himself." Again the Duke's generosity had worked the miracle. During Jeanie's travels David Deans, who had hoped to marry her to the Laird of Dumbiedikes, warmed to the idea of a match between her and Butler. Even his profound religious disagreements with Butler could not blind Davie to a fine son-in-law, especially now that his position was comfortably assured by the Duke's favor.

Butler's ordination, the next milestone in their new life, followed shortly. On the evening of that memorable day, as she looked out over the bay, Jeanie had a secret visit from her sister and George Staunton, now her husband. Effie told her that they were leaving Scotland for an indefinite period, in compliance with the banishment stipulated in her pardon. She would not hear from them again unless they prospered. For five years Jeanie heard nothing. She married Reuben Butler and bore three children at Knocktarlitie vicarage, including a girl whom she christened Euphemia (Effie's full name). Their life was peaceful and spent in the joy of honest toil. Finally a letter from Effie came. It recounted the rapid rise in the fortune and social position of herself and her husband-she was now Lady Staunton of Willingham, a great favorite with London society. But the threat of their dark past and their failure to have children ruled out any chance of personal fulfillment for them. Thereafter Jeanie followed Effie's career through a semi-annual exchange of letters. But time did nothing to improve her sister's despondency.

One day Jeanie found an old broadside-sheet (newspaper) containing the last confession of Meg Murdockson, in which the old hag swore that Effie's child had not died at birth. She sent the document to Effie to make use of as she saw fit. Instead of answering Jeanie's letter, Lady Staunton appeared in person to visit her sister. Meanwhile her husband sought to verify Meg's confession and to reclaim his son, if he proved to be worthy. The search led him from Edinburgh and the scenes of his black past (he found Ratcliffe and Saddletree thriving) right back to Knocktarlitie, where the boy was reported to be in the hands of an infamous outlaw named Donacha Dhu. In Edinburgh Staunton had renewed the acquaintance with Rev. Reuben Butler (who did not, of course, recognized Lord Staunton as Geordie Robertson) and now accompanied him on his way back to the highlands. Shortly after their boat landed they stumbled upon Donacha Dhu and several of his gang. There was a fight and before the bandits could be taken, George Staunton was killed. One of the gang, a lad called "The Whistler," proved to be the very son Staunton had come to fetch. It seemed all too likely that the boy had killed his own father. That night Jeanie went to speak to "The Whistler," who behaved like a savage and escaped by taking advantage of his aunt's compassion. He boarded a ship for America, was enslaved by a Virginia planter, led a revolt against him, and joined a tribe of wild Indians, never to be heard of again. George Staunton, it was revealed at his death, had converted to Catholicism to punish himself for his past wickedness. Ten years after his death, having found little solace in the gay life of London, Effie too embraced the Catholic discipline "and died in severe seclusion" in a foreign convent. "David Deans died full of years and honor," in time to be spared the final **irony** of his grandson's patricide. Reuben and Jeanie "lived beloved, and died lamented."

Comment

Scott's reputation as a novelist today depends almost exclusively upon the Scottish novels. Few writers have equaled his success in capturing the special color and atmosphere of his native land in these fine books. His vivid pictures of Scottish high and lowlife are still valuable as social history, while the "historical" novels, like *Ivanhoe*, are neglected by historians. *The Heart of Midlothian*, set in Edinburgh in the years 1737, is perhaps Scott's greatest single gallery of such pictures. From the elegance of a Queen's country house to the violence of an angry mob of commoners; the teeming streets of Edinburgh to the rugged highlands; dairy farms to tobacco shops; Presbyterian sermons to legal summations - an entire generation of Scottish life is at the fingertips of the reader of this excellent book.

The Heart of Midlothian is also distinguished among the novels for the lucidity and structure of its plot. Too often Scott lapses into awkward flashbacks; too often he bores us with overlong passages; and no one can read the last third of this book without a large measure of indifference as to its outcome. But these are minor faults when we consider the skill with which Scott blends history (The Porteous riots, Queen Caroline, Duke of Argyll) and fiction (Jeanie's story); the single action of the middle chapters; the clear-cut, fully developed **climax** in the trial scene. Certainly *Ivanhoe*, a three- or four-pronged nightmare of construction, cannot compare to the earlier book on the basis of plot.

Characterization is always a problem for Scott. Reuben Butler is a typically water "hero." George Staunton is a Byronic stereotype-burdened with inexpressible guilt, yet proud enough to defy Gods and demons alike. He resembles Bois-Guilbert in Ivanhoe in that he is in love with his own romantic image of himself as a ruined archangel. But beside the realistic characters in this book he seems a hollow invention. Whatever credibility Scott achieves with the young Effie is destroyed by her transformation later in the book. But Jeanie Deans, despite her incredible moral strength (but never quite sanctimoniousness), is a solid heroine. She is also the first lower-class heroine in English fiction who speaks and acts with dignity and intelligence. The minor characters are superb: David Deans, with his home-spun stoicism; the delightfully lampooned Laird of Dumbiedikes; Saddletree, the amateur lawyer and ineffectual know-it-all; Madge Wildfire, the madwoman, at once touching and frightening; the Duke of Argyll-too good to be true: a patriot, a clever and gracious courtier, and a down-to-earth humanitarian, all in one. (In all of these characterizations, incidentally, Scott relies heavily upon dialect.) These eccentrics-each distinct and unusual in his own way, yet fully and concisely defined-are at the summit of Scott's achievement in characterization. Note, however, the echo of certain character relationships from *Ivanhoe*. Like Cedric, David Deans has a marriageable daughter. Her choice is and always has been a young man whose merit is well-known to her father (a son in Ivanhoe, a kind of step-son here), but he persists in hoping for a better match. Cedric promotes a dimwitted blue-blood (Athelstane), as does Deans (Dumbiedikes), each for shallow reasons, only to change their minds for equally shallow reasons later. Neither ever really understands that a humble man of virtue is superior to an aristocratic imbecile; an old man can never learn such things. It is enough that they yield peaceably.

This raises the problem of **theme** in *The Heart of Midlothian*. It is difficult to take seriously Scott's postscript as a statement of the moral significance of the book - any more seriously, let us say, than the humorous tale of Peter Pattieson that frames the novel. The contrast between Butler and Deans, however, points up one legitimate **theme**, familiar to us from our study of Ivanhoe: old ideals must either adjust to modern life or cripple a man for life in this world. David Deans is so unaware of what goes on around him that he is nearly pathetic at times. In matters of religion, his mind is a book that closed over a generation ago. He has raised two girls according to his narrow lights, and both are the worse for it. For all his lofty moral pronouncements he is unable to help Jeanie during her crisis before the trial, and completely incapable of the compassion that might have saved Effie from a second elopement with Staunton. It is not high morals that makes Jeanie a great character but confidence and obstinacy-her ability to do the thing she sets out to do. If she had not had the strength to cancel out the effects of her inflexible moral posture, this might have been a deeper book (See Miss Van Ghent's argument), but it is hardly likely that Scott could then have approved of her so highly or made her so appealing to us. Deans, then, is a lovable old failure. Butler, by comparison, has successfully made his peace with the real world. He can bend his religion when it conflicts with common sense, and he can participate in public affairs when the need arises. Like most of Scott's heroes, he is an unexciting and passive character, but there is no questioning his fitness for modern life.

QUENTIN DURWARD

France in the year 1468 bore little resemblance to the great world power it later became. The illustrious line of strong Bourbon kings that guided France through the two centuries of her greatest glory had not yet appeared. Feudalism and the political disunity it fostered continued to determine the affairs of the land. Many petty dukes and princes governed their domains with absolute authority, and gave only lip-service to the anointed king, Louis XI. Each had his own army, enforced his own laws, and remained substantially independent of the crown. But Louis made it his life's work to change all this. He was a bold and crafty politician, and a ruthless enemy. He dedicated himself to the acquisition of power and, although he was a Christian king, no villainy was too great if it furthered that ambition. The most formidable threat to Louis's dream of uniting France about his throne was Charles the Bold, Duke of Burgandye "then one of the great Princes in Europe." And many lesser tyrants (like William de la March, the Wild Boar of the Ardennes), each strong enough in his own province to range unchallenged there, worked to deepen the divisions in the land and to undermine the power of the king.

This political turmoil inevitably invited large numbers of foreign adventurers to French soil, selling their valuable services to the highest bidder. And no country supplied braver or more loyal warriors than Scotland. One day just such a Scottish knight, Quentin Durward by name, was making his way toward the castle of Louis XI at Plessisles-Tours. He had recently arrived and now sought the advice of an uncle, Ludovic Lely, an Archer in King Louis's Scottish Guard, as to how best to make his fortune in France. His adventures nearly ended before they had begun, however, when he attempted to cross a stream that was deeper than it appeared at first glance. A stout old gentleman, who had been lurking in the bushes nearby with another man, promptly rescued the boy. He identified himself as Maitre Pierre, a silk merchant, and he offered to guide Quentin to the castle. And before he would hear of parting with the lad he invited him to some refreshment at a small inn just outside the castle walls. Quentin's hearty appetite was well-satisfied by the delicacies put before him; but he was even more pleased by the dark-haired beauty who served their wine at Maitre Pierre's command. The two men discussed Quentin's prospects, and when the name of his uncle came up, Maitre Pierre recognized the scarfaced warrior known in France as Le Balafre. He left Quentin at the inn while he went to fetch his uncle from the castle. While Pierre was gone Quentin was charmed by the distant sound of "an air as we are accustomed to suppose flowed from the high-born dames of chivalry, whose knights and troubadours listened and languished." But all Quentin could learn about the singer was that she was lodged in a nearby turret, high above the reach of his vision. Le Balafre arrived and greeted his sturdy nephew warmly. He tried to persuade Quentin to join the Scottish Guards, but the boy had heard too much of King Louis's infamy to relish the thought of serving him. He would decide tomorrow, when he had seen the king at court. Meanwhile Quentin went in search of Maitre Pierre, but no one seemed to have heard of him. These inquiries were cut short by the gruesome sight of a man dangling from a tree in the final agony of his execution. Quentin humanely cut the dead man down, but before he could recover he found himself surrounded by the king's officers. He was astonished to recognize their leader as the companion of Maitre Pierre; but astonishment turned to horror when this officer charged him with interfering with the king's justice and ordered him to be hanged. Only the timely intervention of a passing Scottish archer, shortly reinforced by Le Balafre and some friends, saved Quentin from a painful death. They vouched for the boy's character and loyalty and added that he was one of their company. Quentin's decision had now been made for him; as soon as the Archers returned him to their barracks, therefore, Quentin was introduced to Lord Crawford, Captain of the Scottish Guards, and recruited into their ranks. During a soldier's celebration that evening, Quentin heard his new comrades debating whether the legendary beauty, Countess Isabelle de Croye, had in fact requested Louis's protection and sanctuary in the castle. By this and other evidence they produced, Quentin fancied that the serving-girl at the inn, the singer in the turret, and the Countess were one and the same person. The next day. La Balafre took his nephew to court. He pointed out all the dignitaries before the king at last appeared-better known to Quentin as Maitre Pierre! The king's first act was to walk directly over to Quentin and to pardon him for brawling the day before. But this day held weightier matter for Louis. He granted an audience to the Count de Crevecoeur, Envoy of the Duke of Burgundy. The message he bore demanded, among other things, that Louis surrender the Countess Isabelle de Croye to him immediately, inasmuch as she was the Duke's lawful subject and a particular object of his interest. The Countess, accompanied by her aunt, Lady Hammeline de Croye, had indeed asked and received Louis's aid. Her life in Burgundy had been made insupportable by the Duke's intention to bind her to a political marriage. Louis asked the Envoy to substantiate this grave charge, however, knowing full well that the spy who was the source of this information would never repeat his tale. In fact the spy was the gypsy, Zamet Maugrabin, for whom Louis had been lying in wait when Quentin fell into the stream, and whose body Quentin had cut down the day before. Unable to meet the king's challenge, Crevecoeur complained of foul play and withdrew. That done, Louis proclaimed a boar hunt. Much of the hunt was taken up with political intrigue-Louis was especially interested to know the sympathies of a certain Cardinal Balue. But at one point Louis fell from his horse in pursuit of a wild boar, and only a timely thrust from Quentin's spear saved his life. The new recruit performed one more service when he reported that the Cardinal had been helped onto a horse by Burgundy's ambassador.

After the hunt the king sent his closest adviser, Oliver Dain, to reward Quentin with a full promotion to the rank of Guardsman and to draft him for a dangerous mission. Oliver took him to Roland's Gallery and ordered him to keep watch. As he stood in the empty room he heard the same lute and voice he had heard at the inn. After a time the king personally conducted him to a dining hall and positioned him behind a curtain. His instructions were to arm his cross-bow, train it on the chest of Count de Crevecoeur, and shoot him dead in the event of any aggression against the king's person. Distasteful as it was, Quentin met the test with ease, for the dinner went smoothly and without incident. Now Louis returned his guardsman to the Gallery with orders to allow no man but Oliver Dain or himself to enter that night. Before long, Princess Joan, the king's daughter, appeared; then the Countess Isabelle and her aunt. The latter, Countess Hammeline, complained of Louis's hospitality, unaware that she was speaking to his daughter. But the Princess took no offense and offered her assistance in making their exile more tolerable. Soon another visitor attempted to enter - the Duke of Orleans, Prince Joan's fiancée. Quentin tried to bar him, according to the king's orders, but when the Duke persisted he was no alternative but to let him pass. Orleans greeted all the ladies, but paid particular attention to the young Countess, much to the humiliation of his intended bride. When the king returned and found this group, he berated Quentin for his disobedience: he should have shot any man who refused to respect the king's command. Quentin retired to ponder the events of the evening.

Later that evening Oliver Dain and Louis hit upon a plan to satisfy Burgundy about the refugees and to protect France's best interests. They decided that the Countess Isabelle would certainly have to leave Plessis, but that her marriage to an enemy of Burgundy would spare Louis any dishonor for having turned her out. They would recommend that she and her aunt seek the protection of the Bishop of Liege. Although Liege was a Burgundian town, the route Isabelle would have to take to arrive there passed through the forests where William de la Marck, the Wild Boar of the Ardennes, was strongest. William was a sworn enemy of Burgundy and would hardly let an opportunity like this pass without using it to humiliate the Duke. Indeed he might even be so bold as to marry the Countess, once he had abducted her-especially if Louis were to suggest the idea to him. With the advice and approval of his astrologer, Galeotti Martivale, Louis selected his newest guardsman, Quentin Durward, to escort the ladies on their perilous journey to Liege-a journey he expected to end in the camp of William de la Marck.

The Countess's party, with Quentin at its head, had not traveled far from the castle when it encountered its first mishap. Two strange knights overtook them and demanded that they stop. Quentin unhorsed one of them but could barely hold his own in a pitched sword-battle with the other. Lord Crawford and several of the Scottish Guards arrived just in time to prevent further bloodshed. The fallen knight proved to be the Duke of Orleans, who had conceived this foolhardy means of gaining Isabelle's favor. His companion was Dunois, the greatest champion in France. Crawford arrested both of them and took them to the notorious prison-castle of Loches. After this unpleasantness, the party was joined by a gypsy named Hayraddin Maugrabin (brother of the spy Quentin had cut down), who said he had been commissioned to guide them to Liege. The journey proceeded without incident, except for the trouble Hayraddin's irreverent jests and insults caused every time they stopped overnight at a monastery. Then one evening, at the convent of Namur, Quentin was learning to his dismay of the vulnerability of the Bishop of Liege to the bandits and renegades who roamed his neighborhood (notably Walter de la Marck). In the midst of this disturbing conversation with the Prior, Quentin was informed that Hayraddin had behaved outrageously toward the monks in the convent. Besides spiking their water with spirits, he had ridiculed their patron, St. Francis. The heathen was whipped and driven out of the convent for his offenses. Following a hunch about Hayraddin's strange behavior, Quentin followed the Bohemian into the forest. Hidden behind a willow, he overheard Hayraddin plotting with an agent of William de la Marck to lead their party into an ambush. Hayraddin's only request was that Quentin Durward not be harmed at any time. The next day, without revealing what he knew of Hayraddin's duplicity, Quentin took the women along a different route from the one planned. They by-passed the ambush and arrived safely at the castle of Schonwalt, fortress of the Bishop of Liege.

The burghers of Liege had long been on the verge of open revolt against Burgundy. Their Bishop had been a close friend of his for many years and therefore the Liegeois (i.e. citizens of Liege) regarded him as a puppet, a tool of the Duke's oppression. Conversely, any party opposed to the Duke for whatever reason was considered an ally of the city; King Louis and William de la Marck were included in that company. Quentin appeared in the streets of Liege shortly after having been relieved of his responsibility for the Countess. The journey had been a successful one and his services were no longer needed. The lovesick knight (for such was Isabelle's effect upon him) wandered through Liege, unaware that the uniform of the Scottish guard which he wore had begun to attract attention. Before long he had gathered a crowd of Liegeois about him. They were overjoyed to see this tangible proof that Louis had brought his armies to Liege in support of their anticipated revolt. Before he could correct their hasty conclusions, Quentin found himself being propelled toward the city hall where it was expected he would address the entire citizenry as to the details of his mission. It was plain that his life would be worth little when the true nature of his work was known, so he took the readiest means of escape that presented itself. He confided to the two men who held his arms, Meinheers Rouslaer and Pavillon, that his message was strictly confidential and meant for their ears alone. Instantly the two men ushered him into Pavillon's house (which they happened to be passing at that moment), allowed him to change out of his uniform, and took him back to the castle to await his instructions.

That evening Quentin visited the Bishop's private garden in the hope of seing his beloved Isabelle one more time. His dream seemed to come true when "a female hand" dropped a note down to him from a high window. It was a love letter, encouraging him to persist in his attentions and promising him the fulfillment of his fondest wishes. The brief appearance of Isabelle herself in the garden a few moments later convinced him that his love was reciprocated. In the next few days he plotted to remove her from the dangerous castle and severed his own connections with the wicked King Louis (whose part in this whole scheme he had begun to suspect). On the fourth night Hayraddin stirred him from a sound sleep to announce that the Liegeois, led by

William de la Marck and his men, were marching on the castle. There was not a moment to lose; the women were ready to flee the castle. Together they collected two muffled women and rode away with them into the safety of the darkness. When they were far enough away to be able to rest Quentin discovered that the lady in his arms was not Isabelle, but her amorous aunt, the Countess Hammeline. the note (a little too frank, he had thought at the time) had been hers; and Hayraddin, happy to promote so prosperous a match for the boy, had done his best to bring them together. When the other woman was revealed to be a gypsy servant girl, the incredulous Quentin returned to the castle alone to find his true love.

When he arrived the sack of the city was in full swing. He pretended to be one of the Liegeois and easily regained the turret where he knew Isabelle to be quartered. It was the work of a few moments to find her and to enjoy her embrace. He was fortunate in having encountered and assisted Pavillon on the way to the turret, for the burgess now held the key to their escape. Isabelle disguised herself as Pavillon's daughter, for they would have to pass through the banquet hall in order to leave the castle. This great room had undergone a frightful change since Quentin had seen it last. The savages who fought for William de la Marck had wrecked it with their plundering and carousing. The Wild Boar himself called the good Bishop of Liege before him and butchered him in front of the entire company. What had begun as mild concern among the Liegeois about the coarse manners of William's troops now became a profound dread of the unholy ally they had accepted. Next William tried to intimidate the Liegeois by setting his cutthroats loose among them. But Quentin saved the day by collaring William's own son and holding a dagger at his throat. The Boar called off his men and allowed the Liegeois to go in peace. Quentin Durward and Isabelle spent the remainder of the night at Pavillon's house in the city. In the morning they procured some peasant clothing to disguise themselves and gratefully took leave of the kindly Pavillon and his family.

Not long after they had begun their flight they were pursued by a company of William's soldiers, who chased them directly into the arms of the Count de Crevecoeur's army! Although the Count was a Burgundian, Isabelle far preferred to rely upon the honor of a gentleman than to expose herself to the barbarism of hired murderers. She requested his protection and received it. Quentin asked the Duke whether to consider himself a prisoner, but Crevecoeur was no clearer about that than the young Scot. While Quentin was occupied with his adventures at Liege, King Louis and the Duke of Burgundy had drawn their armies to within striking distance of one another, but as yet no engagement had taken place. Was there a war or not? No one could tell, and Quentin's status therefore remained in doubt. As Crevecoeur drew nearer the city of Peronne (Burgundy's headquarters), however, he was met by two of the Duke's courtiers: Baron d'Hymbercourt and Philip des Comines (the famous historian). They interrupted their sport (falconry) to exchange the latest news with Crevecoeur; theirs was almost as perplexing as his was horrifying: Louis had come to Peronne, accompanied only by a token escort, to negotiate with Burgundy!

All had gone well for Louis before Crevecoeur's return. At the outset he had been accorded the respect proper to his role as titular chief-of-state. Charles, Duke of Burgundy, was a passionate and obstinate man who never forgot an injury, and no man had betrayed him so often and so grievously as Louis. But the world had not often seen a political genius of Louis's caliber. Nothing Charles could say - no reproach or insult - ruffled the king. Instead Louis coolly took advantage of every opportunity to plant the seed of peace and reconciliation in Burgundy's mind.

By now even the chance of an alliance between the two lords and a joint expedition against Louis of Luxembourg (their common enemy and a thorn in the side of France) seemed not altogether out of the question. And Louis's secondary objective of winning the secret regard of some of Burgundy's most important counselors and barons was proceeding nicely. Crevecoeur's news of the revolt and the Bishop's murder, therefore, fell heavily upon Louis's designs. Burgundy had long suspected Louis of inciting the Liegeois to rebellion, and of having formed a secret agreement with William de la Marck to subvert his influence in that area. Now (although Louis had expressly forbidden any action against the Duke during their negotiations at Peronne) it appeared certain that Louis had schemed his last scheme. He was placed under arrest along with his escort and returned to his apartment to await the Duke's judgment.

For all his brilliance as a politician Louis was fanatically superstitious. He wore a hat decorated with statuettes of his favorite saints so that he might pray to the proper one as the occasion demanded. Even more extraordinary was his complete dependence upon the forecasts of his astrologer, Galeotti, in matters of state and private interest. Galeotti had predicted that Quentin Durward's mission would end with honor and advantage to the king. Even the change in Isabelle's route to avoid the ambush had been a fortunate stroke from Louis's point of view, although it deviated from his original plan. Burgundy would certainly not have parleyed with him had the Countess fallen into the hands of William de la Marck. But this time the Scot had failed him. The report of the uprising in Liege that he had given Crevecoeur shattered Louis's dreams and apparently cost him his life. The blame, he reasoned, was Galeotti's. Although a prisoner, Louis was allowed a small body of servants and advisers to attend him. He chose them carefully so that he might arrange Galeotti's summary execution in his own prison cell. This done, he summoned the astrologer and charged him with incompetence. Instead of cowering and begging for mercy, Galeotti scolded the king for having so little faith in the ultimate wisdom of the stars. How else could he himself have learned that his death would precede the king's by just twenty-four hours? The effect of these words was instantaneous, as Galeotti had calculated. The king cancelled the execution plan and dismissed the astrologer; the chance that Galeotti's doom was directly connected with his own was too great a risk to take.

Burgundy meanwhile wrestled with the problem of Louis's fate. His closest advisers, whose respect for the king had risen enormously in the last few days, urged him to be lenient. Crevecoeur went so far as to maintain that Louis knew nothing of the Liege rebellion, and that the Scottish Guardsman, Durward, could testify to this effect. Eager for an end to the affair, the Duke designated the next noon as the time for Louis's hearing. One of the Burgundian counselors who most wished to see Louis's life spared, Philip des Comines, hastened to the king's cell to discuss the prospects for an agreement with Burgundy. Among other concessions, the king gladly disowned his allies in Liege and William de la Marck. One issue on which he was adamant, however, was the marriage between his daughter Joan and the Duke of Orleans. Burgundy preferred to see Orleans married to the Countess Isabelle, but Louis would not endure that humiliation. Comines promptly demonstrated the indifference of a concession on Louis's part. Isabelle, he had learned, would give herself to no man but Quentin Durward. Once more the boy became an asset. Forearmed with the knowledge of Burgundy's demands, Louis prepared for his hearing with characteristic sureness.

The first witness to be called the next day was the Countess Isabelle. Acting on Quentin Durward's instructions, she said nothing that might implicate the king in the misfortunes that had befallen her since leaving Plessis. The boy himself gave a complete and truthful account of the journey to Liege and its consequences, without mentioning his suspicion that the king had masterminded the whole affair. In short, the hearing went so well for Louis that his exoneration was virtually assured. Then fortune turned her wheel once more: a herald from Liege was announced, bearing tidings (Louis presumed) that were certain to link him to the Wild Boar of the Ardennes. Louis rose to the occasion by repudiating William in public and flinging his greetings back in the herald's face. But this was not enough. The herald, who called himself Rouge Sanglier, was in fact our old friend Hayraddin. When he could not decipher a coat-of-arms in heraldic jargon (the usual test of a herald's qualifications), he forfeited his life. His dying request was to speak to Quentin Durward. He made the boy the beneficiary of a vital secret that might make his fortune: William de la Marck planned to deceive Burgundy's troops when they came to retake Liege by attacking their rear with soldiers in French uniforms-a stratagem that might mean complete victory for Louis if he were to follow up this ruse with his own forces. He also had time to deliver a letter for Countess Isabelle from Countess Hammeline, who by now was the bride of the ferocious William de la Marck. By the time Quentin had fetched Hayraddin's horse (he promised to care for it), the resourceful heathen had breathed his last.

Back at Peronne the Duke had called an assembly to witness the betrothal of Countess Isabelle to the Duke of Orleans. She refused the match, however, and Orleans declined to have her by force. Enraged, Burgundy offered her hand to the man who would kill William de la Marck in the forthcoming assault on Liege. Just before the assault on the city Quentin averted any opening for Louis's treachery by revealing to both leaders at once the secret of William's battle plan. During the fighting

Quentin managed to bring the Wild Boar (who, as Hammeline's letter had disclosed and Quentin alone knew, was wearing the uniform of Dunois) to bay. But just when the prize seemed his he heard the wife of his old friend Pavillon calling for help. By the time Quentin had rescued her and returned her intact to her husband, William de la Marck had been slain by another. The lucky blade was Le Balafre, Quentin's uncle; but rather than change the habits of his long life as a single man he passed the honor of Isabelle's hand on to Quentin, whose noble blood and virtue made him a more suitable match. Liege was taken, Louis and Burgundy were temporarily reconciled, and the young Scot and his bride faced a long and happy life together.

Comment

Quentin Durward (1823) is a lively story told with a reasonably well-constructed plot. It is unusual among Scott's novels in that it is set in France, but otherwise it follows fairly closely the pattern of the other historical romances. On the whole, medieval France does not seem a great deal different from medieval England, as Scott conceives of them. Two distinctive features of *Quentin Durward* raise it above the common level of Scott's later novels. The first is the character of King Louis XI-probably Scott's finest historical portrait. Less prominent but ultimately more decisive is the irony and wit of Scott's narrative. Nowhere is Scott's contempt for chivalry more explicit than in this book. Quentin Durward himself is the foil for much of the **irony**: everything he sets his hand to seems to go wrong, but miraculously he prospers. The first time we see him he falls into a stream. Before long he naively cuts down the freshly hanged body of a traitor. The king finds him asleep at the first watch he is ordered to keep, and unable to follow orders at the second. In his first big battle he nearly kills the heir to the throne, and receives a tremendous clout on his skull. He absentmindedly walks through a crowded town wearing an "enemy" uniform, but soon finds himself at the head of a rebellion. The crowning absurdity is his flight from Schonwalt with the wrong Countess, an incident which casts a sarcastic light on the tender scenes of courtly love which preceded it. Quentin even fails to kill William de la Marck although he has the clear and exclusive advantage over his comrades of knowing precisely what disguise William will wear in battle. If these instances of Quentin's haplessness are not indicative enough of Scott's intentions, the following scene should leave little room for doubt. Quentin has been searching for Isabelle during the sack of Schonwalt, but with no success: "He wrung his hands, tore his hair, and stamped on the earth with desperation." He finds a secret door and crashes himself through it with such force that Isabelle, inside the room, swoons with fright. Then:

He hastily raised her from the ground, and joy of joys! it was she whom he sought to save - the Countess Isabelle. He pressed her to his bosom - he conjured her to awake - entreated her to be of good cheer - for that she was now under the protection of one who had heart and hand enough to defend her against armies.

"Durward!" she said, as she at length collected herself, "is it indeed you? - then there is some hope left. I thought all living and mortal friends had left me to my fate - Do not again abandon me!"

"Never - Never!" said Durward. "Whatever shall happen - whatever danger shall approach, may I forfeit the benefits purchased by yonder blessed sign, if I be not the sharer of your fate until it is again a happy one!"

"Very pathetic and touching, truly," said a rough, broken, asthmatic voice behind - "A love affair, I see. . . ."

After the lovers have soared to theatrical eloquence in their professions of attachment and devotion, Pavillon's voice comes like a dash of cold water, or like a pin pricking a balloon. Scott pricks the balloon of starry-eyed idealism and the nonsense it generates wherever he finds it. No **theme** is more congenial to Scott's intelligence or closer to his heart.

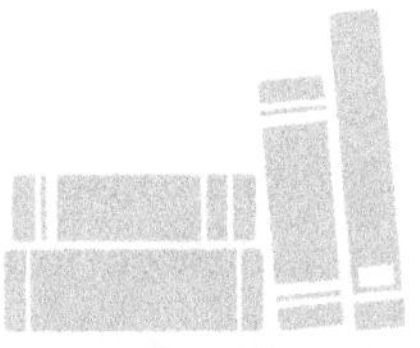

CRITICAL COMMENTARY

The problem in Scott criticism is to explain the decline of the fame and critical reputation of the Waverley Novels since the highwater mark during the nineteenth century. Once Scott was regarded as the greatest English novelist-above Fielding, Jane Austen, Dickens, and George Eliot. Despite the high price of his books Scott's career as a best-selling novelist was phenomenal, and the tide of his popularity continued for two generations after his death. But today his books are considered children's reading and moulder away on shelves of unopened "classics." No responsible modern critic would place him in the first rank of novelists, unless out of respect for his vast influence on better writers.

Yet the astonishing fact is that the flaws and shortcomings that make Scott a second-rate novelist today were perfectly obvious to the best of his contemporaries. Jeffrey, Hazlitt, and Coleridge were among the keenest literary intelligences of the time, and among them they recognized every important complaint that has ever been lodged against Scott's work (the one exception will be mentioned later). Francis Jeffrey, the famous editor of the more famous *Edinburgh Review*, read the first of the *Waverley* novels with such enthusiasm that he broke the Review's policy of excluding novels from its pages. But by the time Ivanhoe appeared he saw full well that Scott's abandonment of Scottish settings and characters spelled trouble for him. Earlier he had noticed the dullness of the hero and heroine, the lovers who occupied the foreground of so many of the *Waverley* novels. But not until *Ivanhoe* did he feel "not only that the characters he brings before us are contrary to our experience, but that they are actually impossible." Indeed, Jeffrey's review marks the first important blow to the reputation of Ivanhoe, the most popular of Scott's novels but seldom a favorite with critics. As early as *Waverley*, Jeffrey anticipated the familiar modern complaint that the novels were "obviously very hastily and in many places unskillfully written." But for all these detractions, Jeffrey thought Scott the greatest genius of his age, "a prodigy of fertility." He praised his Scottish minor characters, his scenes of Scottish life, and his "faithful and animated picture of the manners and state of society." Even before Scott wrote the last of his *Waverley* novels, the "modern" preference for the Scottish novels over the Historical Romances had begun to take shape. Furthermore Jeffrey touched upon a critical issue that still interests us: the persistent **theme** of the *Waverley* novels that grows out of the opposition of two forces in the human personality. In *Waverley* they were "the devoted velour, incorruptible fidelity, patriarchal brotherhood, and savage habits, of the Celtic clans, on the one hand - and the dark, intractable and domineering bigotry of the Covenanters on the other." But as the novels moved farther away from the realities of Scottish life Jeffrey's enthusiasm faded rapidly.

Hazlitt's criticism of Scott is often colored by political motives (Scott was a Tory, or conservative, Hazlitt a radical). But no man wrote more penetratingly and ardently about Scott during the Romantic period. He best of all captures the mood in which the novels were first received: "The novels are like the betrothed of our hearts, bone of our bone, and flesh of our flesh, and we are jealous that any one should be as much delighted or as thoroughly acquainted with their beauties as ourselves . . . What a power is that of genius! What a world of thought and feeling is there rescued from oblivion! How many hours of heartfelt satisfaction has our author given to the gay and thoughtless! How many sad hearts has he soothed in pain and solitude! It is no wonder that the public repay with lengthened applause and gratitude the pleasure they received." Hazlitt locates the important division in Scott's work not between the Scottish novels and the Romances, but between the poetry and the novels. (Scott, remember, had been regarded as England's finest poet.) He even likes "the fine old English Romance of *Ivanhoe.*" But along with Jeffrey he deplored the "innumerable and incessant instances of bad and slovenly English in [the novels], more, we believe than in any other work now printed." Next to Shakespeare (the comparison had begun to intrigue critics) Scott was merely a compiler: "He is Nature's Secretary. He neither adds nor takes away from her book." Where Shakespeare writes, Scott transcribes. Shakespeare's genius is original, Scott's merely derivative: "[Scott's genius] has certain discernible limits; it is strictly national; it is traditional, it relies on actual manners and external badges of character; it insists on costume and dialect; it is one of individual character and situation rather than of general nature." Genius he unmistakably had, but not the creative imagination of the very greatest of writers.

Coleridge was far more critical of Scott than Jeffrey and Hazlitt, but it is not always clear from the letters in which he recorded them how much his opinions are based on mere prejudice. Like the other Romantic poets Coleridge earned little fame and less money for his masterpieces. Worse yet, Scott had "borrowed" some verse from Coleridge without authorization and included it in his highly successful *Lay of the Last Minstrel*. His deduction that Scott's popularity was a sign of his inferiority as an artist, therefore, smells more of envy and personal resentment than sound critical judgment. Yet it is doubtful if a less biased outlook would have changed Coleridge's opinion that Ivanhoe was a "wretched abortion." When his perspective is clearer, however, he brilliantly probes the fundamental mystery of Scott's fame. He finds that the *Waverley* novels appeal to the public because of their subject, "the contrast between the two great problems of social humanity; religious adherence to the past... the desire and the admiration of permanence . . . and the passion for increase of knowledge, for truth in the offspring of reason-in short the mighty instincts of progression and free agency."

The only significant addition to Scott criticism after Coleridge was Thomas Carlyle's famous, essay in the *Westminister Review* of 1838. Like most of his contemporaries Carlyle admired Scott as a man and valued the entertainment his books provided. But he felt Scott had been spoiled by popularity. In particular, the *Waverley* novels were full of diverting comic types and gorgeous tapestries but had nothing in the way of "opinion, emotion, principles, doubts, beliefs." The measure of literature in the Victorian period was "high seriousness" and Scott failed to meet that test. He lacked intelligence, moral significance. In direct contrast to Hazlitt, Carlyle believed "the sick heart will find no healing here; the darkly struggling heart no guidance." Twenty years later, Walter Bagehot (in the *National Review*) wrote a fine analysis of Scott reflecting Carlyle's strictures. Scott's genius was second-rate. He could not write about love, added no depth to his characters, managed plots badly, and failed to convey a clearcut thesis of universal applicability. Bagehot balanced these liabilities against his gifts: sympathy for interesting social types and a Romantic imagination. But it was clear that a new standard of judgment had begun to shift the balance against Scott, even if the reading public did not yet agree. Leslie Stephen added a final insult in his essay on Scott in *Hours in a Library* (1874). He was the first to consign Ivanhoe to the limbo of children's books. Scott's books were without passion, although the Scottish novels were better than the Romances.

The Heart of Midlothian he singles out for special praise, thus setting the trend toward that book's present eminence among the Waverley novels. But on the whole Scott was not substantial enough for a mature audience. Yet these three critics were hardly representative: "The age in general was still warm and tender toward Soott's memory and strongly inclined to consider him the greatest of novelists" (Hillhouse).

By the end of the nineteenth century, however, the magic of Scott's personality had begun to wane. The serious novels of George Eliot, Hardy, and Meredith, novels expressing the deepest philosophical beliefs of their authors, undercut the merely pleasurable Scott. Readers began to find more pertinent and more direct statements about their lives and problems than Scott could offer. Flaubert, Henry James, and E. M. Forster began to restore artistic form and proportion to the novel. And once again the *Waverley* novels suffered greatly by the new standard. As he lost readers, however, Scott acquired ever more strenuous defenders among critics and scholars. Some stressed biography to keep him before the public eye. John Gibson Lockhart had written the definitive Life of Scott, one of the great biographies in English, in 1837-8. Yet John Buchan (1932) and H. J. C. Grierson (1938) reworked much the same material to produce valuable shorter introductions to Scott's life. Others emphasized Scott's influence on others, his place in the history of the novel, or his value as a historian. The debate over whether he was a Romantic still flourishes. General surveys of the novel and literature of the Romantic period are mixed in their appraisal of Scott. E. A. Barker is very warm. He stresses Scott's place in the tradition of the English novel, of course, but also praises his historical imagination and the scope of his characterization. The Waverley novels are "a splendid reconstruction of the past." He compares Scott to Shakespeare without disparagement: "Scott never showed history in the making as Shakespeare did; he chose the exact opposite, to show characters as they were made by history." Philosophically, Scott is a determinist. And his novels reveal the "good-natured mockery of the anti-romantic." T. F. Henderson in the *Cambridge History of English Literature* finds *Ivanhoe,* despite its anachronisms, to reveal a "mastery of manners, customs, and cardinal characteristics of the chivalric past," unmatched by more careful historians. Wilbur L. Cross finds him "a realist when dealing with lowly life; but his prevailing mood was romantic . . . Toward him all the lines of the Romantic revival converge." Beneath the surface of dialect, local color, and romance, Scott's enduring interest is in "human nature, which is practically the same in all times." Lord David Cecil sees his moral view of life as being wider than that of the Victorians, and his imagination "of a finer quality" although less varied and powerful than Dickens's. Certainly not all the general studies are so kind. S. C. Chew is "chilly." Walter Allen threw up over Ivanhoe (in *Six Great Novelists*) but later accorded Scott the genuine compliment that he had grasped "the organic relationships between man and man, man and place, man and society, and man and his past" (in *The English Novel*). The search for new ways to defend Scott's foundering reputation continues up to this very moment. A *London Times Literary Supplement* review of February, 1964, begins with this familiar lament: "No great writer in the history of English literature has fallen into such disrepute as Sir Walter Scott. . . . Not only does his reputation stand low with critics and scholars, he is almost entirely unread by the public." Scott was a "brilliant historian of the seventeenth and eighteenth centuries," the writer goes on, but this is hardly enticing to the general reader. He asks the modern reader to consider instead that *The Heart of Midlothian* was the "first genuinely proletarian [working class] novel in our language." And to those better acquainted with the "craft of fiction" he offers Scott's "astonishing achievement" in portraying simple goodness [in characters like Jeanie Deans] with complete success." But the apologetic tone ("there are other qualities which might conceivably entice . . ."; Scott may be thought worth sampling . . .") of the article confirms the suspicion that Scott's fortunes are at their lowest ebb ever.

Two recent depreciations of Scott are Dorothy Van Ghent's *English Novel* (1953) and Alexander Welsh's *Hero of the Waverley Novels* (1963). Concentrating on the best of the novels, *The Heart of Midlothian,* Miss Van Ghent says that its lack of structure betrays the author's incoherent world view and renders it valueless. She compares it unfavorably with Shakespeare's probing version of a similar **theme** in Measure for Measure. Scott recognizes no moral complexities in the issue: "Sex must be punished, and that is all there is to it." (Cecil had cited this novel as indicative of Scott's broader moral view.) He distracts us from the problem with local color, but this very "deflection of vision is what we mean by disorderliness and disorganization of structure." Welsh's book is less startling because he attacks Scott at one of his well-known weak points: his heroes and heroines. But he is not simply kicking a dead horse. True, these characters are often passive, asexual, and innocent of any action that might be mistaken for real (*Ivanhoe* and Rowena are perfect illustrations). But why has Scott, who could be so deft at characterization, allowed this? Welsh says they are portraits of English gentry, ladies and gentlemen whose livings were secure in the property they inherited and who therefore retired from the active life. They represent the victory of law and property over outdated heroic ideals.

Welsh's conclusion raises the special issue of Scott's underlying theme in the Waverley novels. Different critics have spoken of it in different terms. Jeffrey saw it as the defeat of fading heroic virtues by the bigotry of the present. To Coleridge it was the conservative vs. the progressive, the static vs. the active, the certain comfort of the old vs. the challenge of the new. E. M.

W. Tillyard called it the "need to reconcile the sanguine element in a person with the condition of life actually existing at a given time. To whatever nobility the sanguine element could propel a person, or a people, it could only lead to disaster if it operated in hostile conditions of life." David Daiches, praising the "anti-romantic" fiction of the Scottish novels, finds Scott's **theme** to be "the tragic sense that romantic man must compromise his heroic ideals if he is to survive in the modern world." A fascinating addition to this discussion is Edgar Rosenberg's *From Shylock to Svengali* (1960). His examination of Scott's Jewish characters leads him to conclude that even Ivanhoe is taken up with this **theme** of disillusionment and the hard necessity of shedding outmoded ideals. Scott used "traditional romantic materials . . . to compose an **epitaph** on some of the romantic follies and excesses which, in Ivanhoe, he specifically associated with medieval chivalry." Ivanhoe is a new departure in Scott's career only in the superficial sense that his materials are different. In the more important matter of his ideas and **themes** he is the same rock-ribbed Tory he always was.

The decline in Scott's popularity, then, has not discourage critics and scholars from taking sides in the debate that began with the publication of *Waverley* in 1814. The issues have changed very little. His faults are no more obvious now than they were then. If his virtues no longer outshine his faults it is because they are no longer new or unique. Greater artists have built upon the foundation Scott laid and it is to them and their offshoots that modern readers turn. Scott will never return to his nineteenth century eminence, but as long as men of learning and wisdom differ about his Waverley novels the seeds of revival remain alive.

BIBLIOGRAPHY

General References

James C. Corson, *A Bibliography of Sir Walter Scott*, 1943.

James T. Hillhouse, *The Waverley Novels and their Critics*, 1936.

Biography and Letters

J. G. Lockhart, *Memoirs of the Life of Sir Walter Scott*, 1837-8. Everyman's Library has a one-volume abridgement of this classic of English biography.

H. J. C. Grierson, *Sir Walter Scott*, Bart., 1938.

J. Buchan, *Life of Sir Walter Scott*, 1932.

R. H. Hutton, Scott (*English Men of Letters Series*), 1878. Best short introduction to Scott biography.

H. Pearson, *Walter Scott: His Life and Personality*, 1954.

H. J. C. Grierson, *Letters of Sir Walter Scott*, 1932-7.

General Surveys

W. Allen, *English Novel*, 1954.

E. A. Baker, *History of English Novel*, VI, 1935.

H. A. Beers, *History of English Romanticism in the Nineteenth Century*, 1901.

S. C. Chew, "Nineteenth Century and After," *Literary History of England* (ed. Baugh), 1948.

W. L. Cross, *Development of the English Novel*, 1899.

D. Daiches, *Nineteenth Century Fiction*, 1951.

O. Elton, *Survey of English Literature*, 1780-1830, 1912.

H. N. Fairchild, *The Romantic Quest*, 1931.

L. Stevenson, *The English Novel: a Panorama*, 1960.

E. Wagenknecht, *Cavalcade of the English Novel*, 1943.

Classic Criticism of Scott's Novels

W. Bagehot, "The Waverley Novels," *Literary Studies*, 1858.

J. Brewer, *Shakespeare's Influence on Walter Scott*, 1925.

T. Carlyle, "Sir Walter Scott," in *Critical and Miscellaneous Essays*, 1838.

D. Cecil, *Sir Walter Scott*, 1933.

W. Crockett, *Scott Originals*, 1932.

P. Cruttwell, "Walter Scott," *Pelican Guide to English Literature*, V.

D. Davie, *Heyday of Sir Walter Scott*, 1961.

H. J. C. Grierson, ed., *Sir Walter Scott Lectures*, 1940-8.

W. Hazlitt, "The Spirit of the Age," 1825.

A. Lang, *Introductions to Border ed. of Waverley Novels*, 1902-4.

G. H. Needler, *Goethe and Scott*, 1950.

G. Saintsbury, "The Historical Novel," *Essays in English Literature*, II, 1895.
______, Sir Walter Scott, 1897.

J. C. Shairp, "The Homeric Spirit in Walter Scott," *Aspects of English Poetry*, 1881.

L. Stephen, "Some Words About Sir Walter Scott," *Hours in A Library*, I, 1874.

R. L. Stevenson, "A Gossip on Romance," *Memories and Portraits*, 1887.

E. M. W. Tillyard, *The **Epic** Strain in the English Novel*, 1958.

A. Welsh, *The Hero of the Waverley Novels*, 1963.

C. A. Young, *The Waverley Novels*, 1907.

Ivanhoe

J. E. Duncan, "The Anti-Romantic in *Ivanhoe*," NCF, 1955.

E. A. Freeman, *History of the Norman Conquest*, V.

Maynadier, "*Ivanhoe* and Its Literary Consequences," Essays in *Memory of Barrett Wendell*, 1926.

E. Rosenberg, *From Shylock to Svengali*, 1960.

E. Simon, *The Piebald Standard: a Biography of the Knights Templar*, 1959.

E. Welsford, *The Fool: His Literary and Social History*, 1936.

The Heart of Midlothian

D. Van Ghent, *English Novel: Form and Function*, 1953.

A. Kettle, *Introduction to the English Novel*, 1951.

www.ingramcontent.com/pod-product-compliance
Lightning Source LLC
Chambersburg PA
CBHW071614030726
47598CB00001B/269
9781645424024